Great Source Dailies™
Teacher's Manual

DAILY
Mathematics

Critical Thinking and Problem Solving

Grade
5

GReaT SOuRCe®
EDUCATION GROUP
A Houghton Mifflin Company
New Ways to Know®

CONTENTS

Also Available:

Daily Mathematics Student Book
(sold in packages of 10)

2001 impression

Cover creative and design by Bill SMITH STUDIO. Ron Leighton, Art Director.

Printed in the United States of America

International Standard Book Number: 0-669-48402-4

1 2 3 4 5 6 7 8 9 10 – MZ – 06 05 04 03 02 01

Visit our website: http://www.greatsource.com/

INTRODUCTION

PHILOSOPHY

The Great Source Dailies™ teacher's manuals provide daily review of essential skills. *Daily Mathematics* is based on the principle that all students should have the opportunity to think mathematically every day. Therefore, the problems on these pages emphasize higher-order thinking skills, not drill and practice.

Our goal is for students to discover, through the use of *Daily Mathematics*, that there is more than one way to approach a problem, and that frequently there is more than one correct answer. We hope that students will be rewarded for creativity in their approach to the process of solving problems and that the importance of merely finding "the answer" will be de-emphasized. While doing these problems, of course, students will get plenty of opportunity to practice their arithmetic skills—not only pencil-and-paper skills, but also estimation, mental mathematics, and calculator skills.

We believe that the richness of a student's mathematical experience is enhanced if arithmetic is taught not in isolation and devoid of application, but rather in conjunction with other branches of mathematics and in real-life situations. Therefore, *Daily Mathematics* helps students see connections among various topics—geometry, logic, probability, consumer applications, algebra, number sense, and data analysis—so that the situation is real and, therefore, interesting for students.

Finally, to encourage critical thinking among students, we encourage the teacher to be supportive, not prescriptive. For example, on certain problems, one student might use paper and pencil, another the calculator, and still another, mental mathematics. Instead of considering one approach "right" and the others "wrong," you might discuss with students why they chose the method they used. Similarly, in problems requiring estimation, consider accepting a wide range of answers as "reasonable;" the process is just as important as the result.

HOW TO USE DAILY MATHEMATICS

The program was designed to be used in a variety of ways to suit the preference of the individual teacher. Any of the following approaches, or any combination of them, is workable. The teacher can: write the problem on the chalkboard; present the problem in the Student Book, which provides write-on lines for students; present the problem in a Transparency (available from Great Source, with an Answer Key); or dictate the problem to the students, while putting on the chalkboard any figure or data that is necessary. The teacher can also use the quizzes in the teacher's manual to assess students' success with the problems. Each quiz is comprised of 10 problems from one four-week period.

TIME MANAGEMENT

The problems are designed for 5–10 minutes per day. Due to the richness of some of the problems, as well as the optional follow-up questions provided in some of the teacher's notes, discussion can occasionally proceed well beyond 10 minutes, if you allow it. Some teachers, therefore, might choose to use the program less often than daily and set aside more time, thus reducing the pressure to cut off discussion.

TEACHER'S NOTES

Notes to the teacher are provided alongside every problem for easy reference. The notes include the following:

- A correlation to the *NCTM Standards for School Mathematics* (A summary of each week's correlations is given in the Strands chart on pages 4–5.)

- A pencil icon to indicate a problem whose answer requires writing

- The answer, when there is one correct answer

- Some sample answers when a variety of answers is possible

- Background notes containing useful mathematical or pedagogical information related to the problem

- Occasionally, a related follow-up question to ask students

DAILY MATHEMATICS STRANDS

Students using *Daily Mathematics* are exposed to several important mathematics strands in addition to basic arithmetic skills. These strands, and the weeks in which they appear, are shown in the chart.

	Week																																			
	1	2	3	4	5	6	7	8	9	10	11	12	13	14	15	16	17	18	19	20	21	22	23	24	25	26	27	28	29	30	31	32	33	34	35	36
Numbers and Operations																																				
1.1 Whole-number concepts and operations	•	•	•	•	•	•	•	•	•	•	•	•	•	•	•	•	•	•	•	•	•	•	•	•	•	•	•	•	•			•		•		•
1.2 Fraction concepts and operations			•								•	•	•	•		•		•		•	•	•		•			•		•		•	•		•	•	
1.3 Decimal concepts and operations	•												•				•	•			•		•	•			•	•	•		•		•			
1.4 Number sense	•	•		•	•		•	•	•	•								•		•	•	•	•	•	•	•	•	•	•	•				•	•	•
1.5 Estimation skills and mental computation skills		•									•		•				•			•			•	•			•	•				•		•		•
Algebra																																				
2.1 Patterns and relationships		•	•	•	•	•	•	•	•	•	•	•	•	•	•	•	•	•	•	•	•	•		•		•	•	•	•	•		•		•		•
2.2 Fact families, missing addends, and factors		•		•				•					•		•					•	•		•			•			•			•		•	•	
2.3 Real-number properties	•			•				•	•				•		•		•	•	•	•	•	•	•	•	•	•	•	•	•	•	•	•		•	•	•
2.4 Formulas, expressions, and equations		•	•		•		•	•	•					•			•		•		•	•			•	•	•	•	•			•				
Geometry																																				
3.1 2- and 3-dimensional figures	•		•	•		•	•		•	•	•	•	•	•	•	•	•	•	•	•		•	•		•	•	•	•		•			•		•	•
3.2 Coordinate geometry																•												•								
3.3 Visualization	•							•						•				•	•	•	•		•	•		•		•	•		•			•		•
Measurement																																				
4.1 Units, systems, and processes of measurement		•	•					•	•	•	•	•		•	•	•	•	•	•			•	•	•	•	•	•	•	•		•	•	•		•	•
4.2 Indirect measurements—formulas, proportions, etc.				•		•	•	•					•						•			•	•			•	•		•			•		•	•	•
Data Analysis																																				
5.1 Data collection, organization, and display			•				•				•						•					•				•						•	•			
5.2 Data analysis using the mean, median, mode, and range	•			•			•														•			•								•			•	
5.3 Probability concepts					•											•	•												•			•				

Daily Mathematics Strands *continued*

Week

	1	2	3	4	5	6	7	8	9	10	11	12	13	14	15	16	17	18	19	20	21	22	23	24	25	26	27	28	29	30	31	32	33	34	35	36
Problem Solving																																				
6.1 Choosing the operation			•	•		•			•	•								•	•	•		•								•		•		•		
6.2 Solving multi-step problems			•	•	•	•	•	•	•		•		•					•			•	•	•	•		•	•			•	•		•		•	•
6.3 Using tables, lists, graphs, patterns, diagrams or models		•	•	•	•	•		•	•		•	•	•	•	•	•	•	•	•	•	•	•	•	•	•	•	•	•	•	•	•	•	•	•	•	
6.4 Working backward or using guess-and-check	•	•	•	•		•	•	•			•		•	•		•		•					•						•		•	•		•	•	
Reasoning and Proof																																				
7.1 Proportional reasoning	•					•						•					•	•				•		•				•	•	•	•		•		•	•
7.2 Making and investigating conjectures	•				•		•	•	•		•		•		•	•	•	•	•	•	•	•	•	•	•					•		•		•		•
7.3 Making and evaluating math arguments		•	•		•	•		•	•	•	•			•		•	•				•	•				•			•	•	•		•		•	
Communications																																				
8.1 Communicating math thinking clearly	•	•	•	•	•	•		•	•				•	•	•		•	•	•		•	•	•	•	•			•	•	•			•			•
8.2 Using language of math precisely	•		•			•				•	•				•			•			•		•	•	•		•	•		•			•			•
Connections																																				
9.1 To other math topics	•	•	•	•	•	•	•	•	•	•	•		•	•	•		•	•					•			•		•	•	•	•	•		•	•	
9.2 To other subject areas				•		•							•	•					•									•		•				•		
Representations																																				
10.1 Modeling physical, social, and math ideas using math symbols		•	•	•	•	•	•		•	•		•		•	•	•		•	•	•	•	•	•	•	•	•	•	•	•		•	•	•			•
10.2 Translating among representations		•			•	•					•				•						•							•	•		•		•			•
10.3 Writing and modeling whole numbers, base-10 numerals, fractions, decimals, and integers	•		•								•			•	•		•		•	•	•		•		•	•		•		•	•			•	•	

SKILLS COVERED	DAILY PROBLEMS	TEACHER NOTES WITH ANSWERS
1 **Numbers and Operations** 1.1 **Communications** 8.1 **Connections** 9.1	A digital clock shows either 3 digits or 4 digits at a time. At what time do the digits have the greatest sum? Explain how you found your answer.	9:59 At 9:59 the sum of the digits is 23. Students who answer 12:59 may be assuming that the sum of any four numbers is greater than the sum of three numbers. Explanations will vary. Students will probably note that their choices of numerals were limited to those which could possibly appear on a clock.
2 **Numbers and Operations** 1.3 **Communications** 8.2 **Representations** 10.3	Write in standard form. 1. One hundred seven thousandths 2. One hundred and seven thousandths	**1.** 0.107 **2.** 100.007 Stress the importance of the word *and* for placement of the decimal point.
3 **Numbers and Operations** 1.1, 1.4 **Algebra** 2.3 **Reasoning and Proof** 7.2	Find a number that results in a greater number when it is added to 100 than when it is multiplied by 100.	Answers will vary. Possible answers: $^-1$; 0; $\frac{2}{3}$; 1 Any number less than $1\frac{1}{99}$ will work. If students give an answer of 0 or 1, you may want to take the opportunity to review the Additive Identity Property of 0, $a + 0 = a$, and the Multiplicative Identity Property of 1, $a \times 1 = a$.

✎ Answer requires writing.

SKILLS COVERED	DAILY PROBLEMS	TEACHER NOTES WITH ANSWERS

4

Numbers and Operations 1.1, 1.4
Problem Solving 6.4
Reasoning and Proof 7.1, 7.2

The sum of Mary's age and her mother's age is 36.
Mary's mother is five times older than Mary.

How old is each person?

Mary is 6, and her mother is 30.

You may want to suggest that students use the guess-and-check approach to solve this problem. Suggest that students keep an organized list of their guesses.

Numbers that have a sum of 36:	Is one number 5 times the other?
1, 35	No
2, 34	No
3, 33	No
4, 32	No
5, 31	No
6, 30	Yes

5

Geometry 3.1, 3.3
Connections 9.1

This pattern can be folded to make a cube.

If the 6 is to be on the top of the cube, what number will be on the bottom?

```
        +---+
        | 1 |
+---+---+---+
| 2 | 3 | 4 |
+---+---+---+---+
        | 5 | 6 |
        +---+---+
```

3

If students are having trouble visualizing the pattern folded as a cube, have them make a sketch of the pattern, cut it out, and fold it.

DAILYMathematics

	SKILLS COVERED	DAILY PROBLEMS	TEACHER NOTES WITH ANSWERS
6	**Numbers and Operations** 1.5 **Reasoning and Proof** 7.3 **Communications** 8.1 **Representations** 10.1	Mr. Tron's fifth-grade class collected about 100 cans for the food drive. Ms. Sander's fifth-grade class collected about 200 cans. The principal stated that the two fifth-grade classes collected about 400 cans. Explain how the principal could have made this statement.	*Answers will vary. Possible answer:* The sum of two numbers that round down can equal an amount that rounds up. If students are having difficulty understanding this, give them several examples, such as Mr. Tron's class collected 145 cans (rounds to 100), and Ms. Sander's class collected 225 cans (rounds to 200). The total collected is 370 cans (rounds to 400).
7	**Numbers and Operations** 1.1, 1.4 **Algebra** 2.2, 2.4 **Problem Solving** 6.4	Find a 2-digit number that is equal to three times the product of its digits.	15 or 24 Students can narrow down the possibilities by realizing that the number must be a multiple of 3. Suggest that students use the guess-and-check strategy to solve this problem.
8	**Measurement** 4.1 **Problem Solving** 6.3 **Representations** 10.1	Jake plans to make 12 cuts in a board. There will be a 10-inch interval between cuts. How long is the board?	130 in., or 10 ft 10 in. Suggest that students draw a sketch of the board and the cuts to see that the number of 10-inch intervals is one more than the number of cuts. If necessary, explain that the 12 cuts are in addition to the cuts that formed the ends of the board.

Answer requires writing.

SKILLS COVERED	DAILY PROBLEMS	TEACHER NOTES WITH ANSWERS

9

Numbers and Operations 1.1
Algebra 2.1
Problem Solving 6.3
Connections 9.1

A cuckoo clock cuckoos once at 1 o'clock, twice at 2 o'clock, three times at 3 o'clock, and so forth.

How many times does it cuckoo each day?

156 times

$[2 \times (1 + 2 + 3 + 4 + 5 + 6 + 7 + 8 + 9 + 10 + 11 + 12)]$

$6 \times 13 = 78$
$2 \times 78 = 156$

You may want to suggest that students use the pairing method to find the sum of consecutive numbers. You can extend this problem by asking students to find the sum of the numbers from 1 through 100.

$(5,050; 50 \times 101 = 5,050)$

10

Data Analysis 5.2
Problem Solving 6.3
Representations 10.2

1. What was Company B's most profitable year?
2. What is the average profit for the years shown?
3. In which year did the company have profits that were below average?

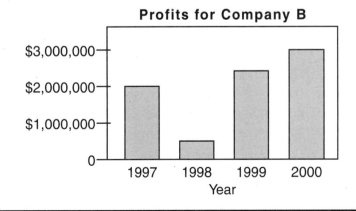

Profits for Company B

1. 2000
2. $2,000,000
3. 1998

Students may need to be reminded that the average is computed by adding together the profits for the 4 years, then dividing by 4. You may want to mention that the *average* is also referred to as the *mean*.

SKILLS COVERED	DAILY PROBLEMS	TEACHER NOTES WITH ANSWERS
11 **Algebra** 2.4 **Reasoning and Proof** 7.3 **Connections** 9.1	Lerna has two coins that total 30¢. What are the two coins if one coin is not a nickel?	A quarter and a nickel One coin is not a nickel, but the other one is!
12 **Numbers and Operations** 1.2 **Problem Solving** 6.1, 6.2, 6.4 **Representations** 10.1	Juan gave two thirds of his baseball card collection to his best friend, Marcus. He gave one half of the cards he had left to his brother. Finally, he gave one half of the cards he had left to his sister. He had 25 cards left. How many cards did Juan originally have in his collection?	300 cards You may suggest that students work backward to solve this problem. The 25 cards Juan had left represent half of what he had (50 cards) before giving cards to his sister. The 50 cards represent half of what Juan had (100 cards) before giving cards to his brother. The 100 cards represent one third of what Juan had originally.
13 **Numbers and Operations** 1.1 **Measurement** 4.1 **Problem Solving** 6.2, 6.4 **Connections** 9.1	Jesse is 60 inches tall. That is 10 inches taller than Marie. The difference between Joe's height and Jesse's height is 2 inches more than between Joe's height and Marie's height. How tall are Marie and Joe?	Marie: 50 in.; Joe: 54 in. Students can determine Marie's height using the information in the first two sentences of the problem. Then, by using the guess-and-check strategy, they can find Joe's height from the information in the third sentence.

SKILLS COVERED	DAILY PROBLEMS	TEACHER NOTES WITH ANSWERS

14

Algebra 2.1
Problem Solving 6.3
Communications 8.1, 8.2
Representations 10.3

How many different 3-digit numbers can you write using the digits 0, 2, 4, and 6? Use a digit only once in a number. Explain your method for finding the answer.

18 numbers

Students may choose to make an organized list or use patterns. They should note that 3 out of the 4 numbers can be used in the hundreds place; 3 out of the 3 remaining numbers can be used in the tens place, and 2 out of the 2 remaining numbers can be used in the ones place. Therefore, there are $3 \times 3 \times 2$, or 18, possible numbers.

246	206	402	624	604
264	260	420	642	640
204	426	406	602	
240	462	460	620	

You may want to extend this problem by asking students how many different 3-digit numbers can be made from any 4 nonzero digits, using each number only once. (24; $4 \times 3 \times 2 = 24$)

15

Geometry 3.1
Communications 8.1

Which figure can you draw without lifting your pencil or retracing a line? Show how you do it.

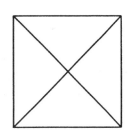
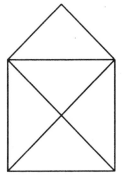

The second figure; Answers will vary. *Possible answers:*

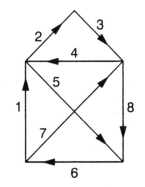
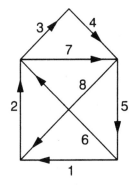

You may want to challenge students to make up their own figures and have their classmates try to redraw them using the same rules.

DAILYMathematics

SKILLS COVERED	DAILY PROBLEMS	TEACHER NOTES WITH ANSWERS

16
Numbers and Operations 1.1
Algebra 2.1
Problem Solving 6.3
Representations 10.1

Chantel made a display of video-game cartridges. There are 3 games in the top row. There are 3 more cartridges in each row than in the row above it.

If the display has 8 rows, how many cartridges did Chantel use?

108 cartridges

$3 + 6 + 9 + 12 + 15 + 18 + 21 + 24$

$4 \times 27 = 108$

You may want to hint that the *pairing method* introduced on Day 9 may also be applied to this problem.

17
Algebra 2.1
Data Analysis 5.1
Problem Solving 6.3
Representations 10.1

Marcie, Duane, Kari, and Michael are sitting around a table. Kari is sitting across from Marcie. Marcie is sitting at Duane's right.

Who is seated at Michael's left?

Marcie

Students may find it helpful to write each person's name on a piece of paper and arrange the names using the given clues.

Kari

Duane   Michael

Marcie

18
Numbers and Operations 1.4
Problem Solving 6.1, 6.2
Communications 8.1
Representations 10.1

Kevin, José, and Marissa decided to share equally the cost of a present for their friend. Kevin spent $7, José spent $3, and Marissa spent $2.

How much did each person pay the others so that everyone spent the same amount? Explain how you solved the problem.

José paid Kevin $1 and Marissa paid Kevin $2.

Encourage students to solve this problem using mental computation. Kevin, José, and Marissa spent a total of $12. Divided evenly, each person's share is $4. Therefore, Kevin needs to be paid $1 from José and $2 from Marissa.

Answer requires writing.

SKILLS COVERED	DAILY PROBLEMS	TEACHER NOTES WITH ANSWERS

19

Geometry 3.1
Problem Solving 6.3, 6.4
Connections 9.1

Divide a clock face into three parts using two straight lines so that the sum of the numbers in each part is 26.

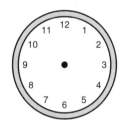

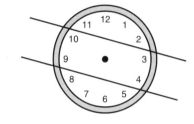

You may want to suggest that students try the guess-and-check method.

20

Numbers and Operations 1.1, 1.4
Algebra 2.1, 2.2
Problem Solving 6.2

Arrange each of the numbers 10, 12, 13, 14, and 16 in the empty circles so the sum of the numbers along each straight line is 32.

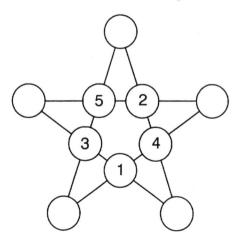

By subtracting the given numbers in each line from 32 and using number sense, students will be able to easily eliminate choices.

This activity can be extended by asking students to determine 5 numbers that can be used to complete this puzzle for a different given sum. (Any 5 numbers following the pattern n, $n + 2$, $n + 3$, $n + 4$, and $n + 6$ will work.)

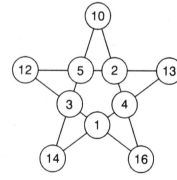

 You may wish to use the standardized-test format found at the back of this manual as a review or testing option.

	SKILLS COVERED	DAILY PROBLEMS	TEACHER NOTES WITH ANSWERS
21	**Problem Solving** 6.3 **Connections** 9.1 **Representations** 10.1, 10.2	Tell whether the angle formed by the hands of a clock will be 90°, less than 90°, or greater than 90° at each of the following times: **1.** 3:30 **2.** 12:45 **3.** 6:15	**1.** Less than 90° **2.** Greater than 90° **3.** Greater than 90° Students may need to be reminded that a 90° angle is a right angle, and that as a minute hand moves around a clock face, the hour hand advances also, to the next hour. A physical model of a clock may help students who have trouble visualizing the relationships of the hands.

22	**Numbers and
	   Operations** 1.1, 1.4
	Algebra 2.3
	Reasoning and Proof 7.3
	Communications 8.1
		Choose the correct answer without working the problem. Explain.
		
		    $327 \div 6 =$
		
		54 R3 54 R6 55 R7 55 R9
			54 R3
			Students should note that all other remainders are greater than or equal to the divisor.

23	**Algebra** 2.1 **Problem Solving** 6.3 **Representations** 10.1	At Mom's Restaurant, a customer gets a free lunch after paying for 6. Carolyn ate lunch at Mom's 50 times last year. How many of those lunches were free?	7 lunches, if the first lunch of the year was paid for, or 8 lunches, if the first lunch of the year was free because it was earned the previous year

SKILLS COVERED	DAILY PROBLEMS	TEACHER NOTES WITH ANSWERS

24   **Numbers and Operations** 1.1
Algebra 2.4
Problem Solving 6.2, 6.3
Connections 9.2

In professional football, a team can score in the following ways:

Type of Play	Points
Touchdown	6
Field goal	3
Safety	2
Point after touchdown	1

During a game a team scores a total of 20 points.
They score 2 touchdowns.

In what ways could they have scored the remaining points?

This organized list shows the possible combinations of other plays the team could have made.

Field goals	Safeties	Points after touchdown
2	1	0
2	0	2
1	2	1
0	4	0
0	3	2

Students may notice that certain combinations of plays are not possible since only 2 touchdowns were scored. This makes 2 the maximum number of points after touchdown.

---

25   **Measurement** 4.2
Data Analysis 5.3
Reasoning and Proof 7.2

1. What number are you most likely to land on if you spin the spinner?

2. How could you change the spinner to make the chance of landing on 1, 2, or 3 equal?

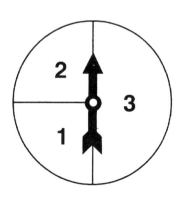

1. 3

2. Answers will vary. *Possible answers:*

	SKILLS COVERED	DAILY PROBLEMS	TEACHER NOTES WITH ANSWERS

26   **Numbers and Operations** 1.1
Algebra 2.1
Reasoning and Proof 7.3
Communications 8.1

Write the next number in the pattern. Explain.

1. 8, 12, 10, 14, 12, 16, 14, _____

2. 2, 6, 3, 9, 6, 18, 15, _____

1. 18; Add 4, subtract 2.
2. 45; Multiply by 3, subtract 3.
Any other explanation that students can justify is acceptable.

---

27   **Numbers and Operations** 1.1
Data Analysis 5.2

Dustin bowled games with scores of 120, 116, and 127.

What was his average?

121
You may need to remind students that the *average* is found by adding the three numbers and dividing the sum by 3. The *average* is also referred to as the *mean*.

---

28   **Algebra** 2.4
Problem Solving 6.1, 6.4
Connections 9.1
Representations 10.1

A pencil and an eraser cost 40¢.

If the pencil costs 30¢ more than the eraser, what is the cost of the eraser?

5¢
Students may incorrectly solve this problem by subtracting the two given amounts. Encourage students to always check their answers. This is another problem to which students can apply the guess-and-check strategy.

SKILLS COVERED	DAILY PROBLEMS	TEACHER NOTES WITH ANSWERS

29

Numbers and Operations 1.1
Problem Solving 6.2, 6.3, 6.4
Communications 8.1

There were 36 heads and 104 legs in a group of horses and riders.

How many horses were in the group?
How many riders were in the group?
Explain how you found your answer.

16 horses, 20 riders

Students may say they used an organized list like the one below to apply the guess-and-check strategy to this problem.

Numbers whose sum is 36	Number of horses	Number of horses' legs	Number of riders	Number of riders' legs	Total legs
12, 24	12	48	24	48	96
15, 21	15	60	21	42	102
16, 20	16	64	20	40	104

This problem previews solving a system of equations in two variables.

30

Geometry 3.1
Problem Solving 6.3
Representations 10.2

How many small cubes are in this block?

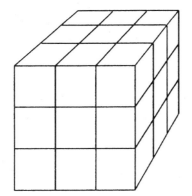

27 cubes

If students are having difficulty visualizing the 27 cubes, have them build the figure shown using centimeter cubes. Then have them count the number of centimeter cubes they used.

SKILLS COVERED	DAILY PROBLEMS	TEACHER NOTES WITH ANSWERS

31

Numbers and Operations 1.1
Geometry 3.1
Measurement 4.1
Problem Solving 6.2
Representations 10.1

What is the area of a square whose perimeter is 24 inches?

36 square inches

You may need to remind students that the sides of a square are equal in length. Since the length of each side of this square is 6 inches, the area is 36 square inches. Check that students express the answer in square inches.

32

Geometry 3.3
Measurement 4.1, 4.2
Connections 9.1
Representations 10.1

A clock has marks indicating 5-minute intervals, but no numbers. Reflected in a mirror, it reads 5:20.

What time is it really?

6:40

This problem focuses on the geometric concept of *reflection*.

Extend this problem by asking students when the time shown in the mirror and the actual time would be the same. (12:00, 6:00)

33

Numbers and Operations 1.1, 1.4
Problem Solving 6.4
Reasoning and Proof 7.1
Communications 8.1, 8.2

What three consecutive even numbers have a sum of 738?
Explain how you found your answer.

244, 246, and 248

Students will probably use the guess-and-check strategy to solve this problem. Students may notice that if they divide 738 by 3, they can find the middle number. Then since these are consecutive even numbers, they can subtract 2 to find the first number and add 2 to find the third.

Answer requires writing.

SKILLS COVERED	DAILY PROBLEMS	TEACHER NOTES WITH ANSWERS

34

Numbers and Operations 1.1
Algebra 2.1
Reasoning and Proof 7.2
Connections 9.2
Representations 10.1

A package of plastic forks contains 8 forks. A package of plastic knives contains 12 knives.

What is the fewest number of packages you would have to buy to have exactly the same number of forks as knives?

Three packages of forks and 2 packages of knives

If students have not learned to find least common multiples, suggest that they solve this problem by making two tables, one that displays multiples of 8 and another that displays multiples of 12.

Number of packages	1	2	3	4
Number of forks	8	16	24	32

Number of packages	1	2	3	4
Number of knives	12	24	36	48

35

Geometry 3.1, 3.3
Representations 10.1

Remove two toothpicks so that the diagram shows only two squares.

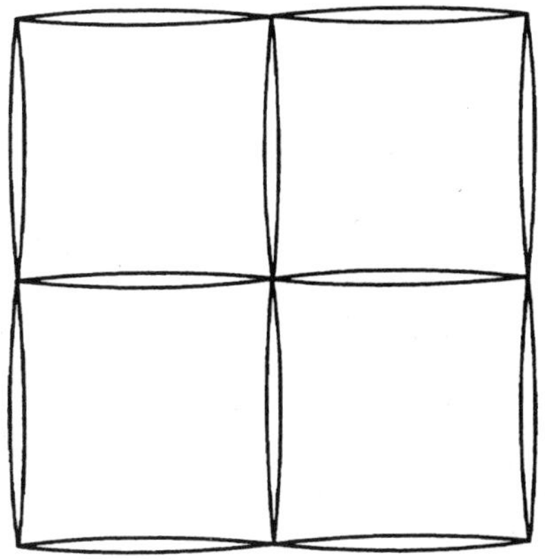

This diagram shows two squares after two toothpicks have been removed. Placement of the inner square may vary.

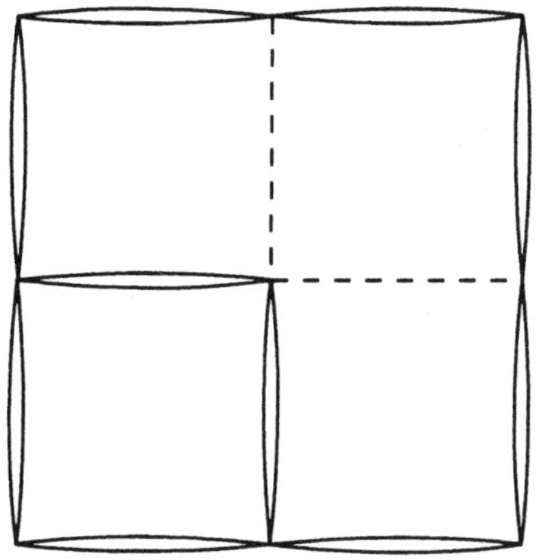

SKILLS COVERED	DAILY PROBLEMS	TEACHER NOTES WITH ANSWERS

36   **Geometry** 3.1
Measurement 4.1, 4.2
Reasoning and Proof 7.3
Communications 8.1

Can you draw a triangle that has sides that are 2 inches, 3 inches, and 10 inches? Explain.

No; In a triangle, the sum of the lengths of any two sides must be greater then the length of the third side.

If students are having difficulty visualizing this, have them attempt to draw the triangle in the problem. First have them draw a 10-in. line. Then have them try to complete the triangle by drawing a 2-in. and a 3-in. line from either end of the 10-in. line. You may want to extend this problem by asking students to draw a triangle that has sides that are 6 in., 8 in., and 10 in.

---

37   **Algebra** 2.1
Data Analysis 5.1
Problem Solving 6.3
Reasoning and Proof 7.2
Connections 9.1

Bob, Tyrone, Maria, Jason, and Rosa are all different ages.
Maria is older than Bob and younger than Tyrone.
Jason is older than Tyrone.
Rosa is older than Bob and younger than Maria.

List the names of the five people, from oldest to youngest.

Jason, Tyrone, Maria, Rosa, Bob

You may suggest that students write the names of the five people on small pieces of paper and move them around according to the description in the paragraph. Or you may want to choose five students to enact the situations.

---

38   **Numbers and**
    Operations 1.1, 1.4
Data Analysis 5.2
Problem Solving 6.2, 6.4
Communications 8.1

The Wildcats' average score for three basketball games is 76.
They scored 70 and 84 in the first two games.

What score did they have in the third game?
Explain how you found the answer.

74

This problem can be solved by working backward through the method for finding averages. Since the average of 3 scores is 76, the sum of the scores must be 3 × 76, or 228. So, the score of the third game is 228 – (70 + 84), or 228 – 154, which is 74.

Answer requires writing.

SKILLS COVERED	DAILY PROBLEMS	TEACHER NOTES WITH ANSWERS

39

Numbers and Operations 1.1, 1.4
Algebra 2.1
Problem Solving 6.3
Reasoning and Proof 7.2
Connections 9.1

Yani has between 50 and 100 pennies in her collection. When she divides them into groups of 2, of 3, or of 7, there is always 1 penny left.

How many pennies does Yani have in her collection?

85 pennies

Students can solve this problem by listing all the numbers between 50 and 100 that result in a remainder of 1 when divided by 2, by 3, and by 7.

2: 51, 53, 55, . . . , 99
3: 52, 55, 58, . . . , 97
7: 57, 64, 71, . . . , 99

The only number that would appear in all three lists is 85.

This problem can also be solved by finding the least common multiple of 2, 3, and 7, which is 42. The number of pennies in the collection would have to be a multiple of 42 plus 1. The only such number between 50 and 100 is 85.

40

Algebra 2.1, 2.4

A teacher asked students to name numbers. After each number, the teacher responded using a certain rule. This table shows the numbers named by the students and the teacher's responses.

Student input	1	2	3	4	5	6	7
Teacher response	3	3	5	4	4	3	5

What rule did the teacher use?

The teacher wrote the number of letters in the word for the number named by the students.

If your students do not discover the rule the first day, you may want to leave this problem displayed for several days and add more input and responses each day, such as: input 1,000, response 11. This problem previews the concept of functions.

You may wish to use the standardized-test format found at the back of this manual as a review or testing option.

SKILLS COVERED	DAILY PROBLEMS	TEACHER NOTES WITH ANSWERS

41   **Algebra** 2.1
Communications 8.1
Representations 10.1

Sarah went to bed at 8:00. Her alarm clock was set for 9:00.

How much sleep could Sarah get before her alarm would wake her up?
Explain your answer.

1 hour or 13 hours, depending on whether the clock distinguishes between A.M. and P.M. Unless stated, this could not be assumed.

---

42   **Algebra** 2.1
Problem Solving 6.3
Reasoning and Proof 7.3
Communications 8.1
Representations 10.1

At a red light, 2 cars are stopped in front of a car, and 2 cars are stopped behind a car.

What is the fewest number of cars that could be stopped at the red light?
Make a drawing to explain your answer.

3 cars

You may need to point out that the same car can be included in more than one description.

---

43   **Numbers and
     Operations** 1.1, 1.4
Algebra 2.4
Problem Solving 6.1, 6.2

Insert + or − symbols to make each number sentence correct.

1. 3 2 5 4 2 2 = 6

2. 8 4 3 5 2 1 = 7

3. 4 2 5 7 8 4 = 8

4. 2 1 3 5 9 7 = 9

Answers may vary. A possible answer for each is given.
1. $3 - 2 + 5 + 4 - 2 - 2 = 6$
2. $8 + 4 - 3 - 5 + 2 + 1 = 7$
3. $4 + 2 + 5 - 7 + 8 - 4 = 8$
4. $2 + 1 + 3 + 5 - 9 + 7 = 9$

By the order of operations, addition and subtraction should be performed in the order in which they occur, from left to right.

✎ Answer requires writing.

SKILLS COVERED	DAILY PROBLEMS	TEACHER NOTES WITH ANSWERS

44

Numbers and Operations 1.1, 1.4
Algebra 2.4
Problem Solving 6.2
Communications 8.1

Haki has an odd number of stamps in his collection. The sum of the digits in the number of stamps he has is 12. The hundreds digit is three times the ones digit.

If he has between 1,000 and 2,000 stamps in his collection, how many stamps does Haki have? Explain how you found the answer.

1,371 stamps

This problem can be solved using number sense. The number is between 1,000 and 2,000, so the thousands digit must be 1, and the sum of the other three digits must be 11.

If the hundreds digit is three times the ones digit, the hundreds and ones digits must be 0 and 0, 3 and 1, 6 and 2, or 9 and 3. The number is odd, so the ones digit cannot be 0 or 2.

If the hundreds digit and the ones digit are 9 and 3, their sum is greater than 11. So, the hundreds and the ones digits must be 3 and 1, and the tens digit must be 11 − (3 + 1), or 7.

45

Geometry 3.1
Measurement 4.1, 4.2
Reasoning and Proof 7.2
Connections 9.1

Each of the three rectangles is the same shape and size.

Find the perimeter of the figure.

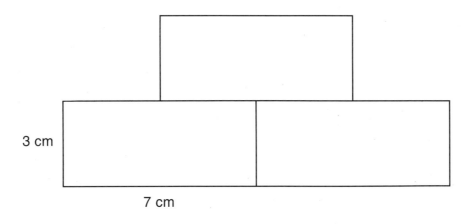

3 cm

7 cm

40 cm

You may need to point out that the distance across the top of the rectangles is the same as the distance across the bottom.

Perimeter = 3 cm + 3 cm + 3 cm + 3 cm + 7 cm + 7 cm + 7 cm + 7 cm, or 40 cm.

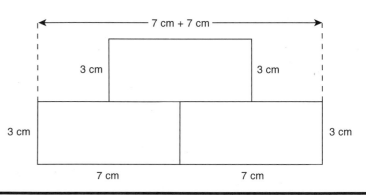

7 cm + 7 cm

3 cm   3 cm

3 cm   3 cm

7 cm   7 cm

✎ Answer requires writing.

SKILLS COVERED	DAILY PROBLEMS	TEACHER NOTES WITH ANSWERS
46 **Numbers and Operations** 1.1 **Algebra** 2.4 **Reasoning and Proof** 7.3 **Connections** 9.1 **Representations** 10.1	Sylvia has 8 coins that total 74¢. Will she be able to use the exact-change lane at a highway toll booth that requires 30¢? Explain how you know.	No. Because Sylvia has 74¢, 4 coins have to be pennies. The remaining coins add to 70¢. The only way to reach 70¢ with exactly 4 coins is with 2 quarters and 2 dimes. Exactly 30¢ cannot be made with any combination of these coins.
47 **Numbers and Operations** 1.1 **Algebra** 2.2, 2.3 **Problem Solving** 6.1 **Reasoning and Proof** 7.2	When doing some math homework, Fred made up the symbol . Part of his work looked like this: 8 = 32 △• 0 = 0 △• 1 = 4 What could △• mean?	△• could mean "multiply by 4." Students may come up with other possibilities. Accept any answer that students can justify.
48 **Numbers and Operations** 1.1, 1.4 **Algebra** 2.1 **Representations** 10.1	The number of students on the field trip is greater than 30 but less than 50. When seated 2 in a seat on the bus, no student has to sit alone. When placed in groups of 5 for a tour, all groups are the same size. How many students are on the field trip?	40 students This problem can be solved using number sense. Since the students can be divided into groups of 5, the number of students must be 35, 40, or 45. All students can be seated in pairs, so the number of students must be even. Since 35 and 45 are odd numbers, the number of students on the field trip must be 40.

Answer requires writing.

SKILLS COVERED	DAILY PROBLEMS	TEACHER NOTES WITH ANSWERS

49

Numbers and Operations 1.2
Problem Solving 6.2
Communications 8.2
Representations 10.1

Kyle had 7 eggs. He used half of these plus $\frac{1}{2}$ egg to make an omelet.

He used half of what was left plus $\frac{1}{2}$ egg to make a batch of cookies.

Then he used half of what was left plus $\frac{1}{2}$ egg to make a meat loaf.

How many eggs did Kyle use for each thing he made?

Kyle used half of 7, or $3\frac{1}{2}$, plus $\frac{1}{2}$, or 4 eggs, to make the omelet. 7 − 4, or 3 eggs, were left. He used half of 3, or $1\frac{1}{2}$, plus $\frac{1}{2}$, or 2 eggs to make the cookies. 3 − 2, or 1 egg was left. He used half of 1, or $\frac{1}{2}$, plus $\frac{1}{2}$, or 1 egg to make the meat loaf.

50

Numbers and Operations 1.1, 1.4
Geometry 3.1
Measurement 4.1
Connections 9.1

Find the perimeter and the area of this figure. Explain how you found your answer.

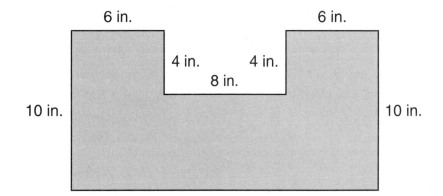

Perimeter: 68 in.; Area: 168 in.

The base of the figure is 6 in. + 8 in. + 6 in. = 20 in., so to find the perimeter, add 20 to the sum of all the other lengths shown.

To find the area, divide the figure into three rectangles, and find the sum of the areas. The division can be made two ways: two 10-in. by 6-in. rectangles and one 6-in. by 8-in. rectangle, or two 4-in. by 6-in. rectangles and one 6-in. by 20-in. rectangle. Students can also find the area of the complete 10-in. by 20-in. rectangle, then subtract the missing area, which is 4 in. by 8 in.: 200 in. − 32 in. = 168 in.

SKILLS COVERED	DAILY PROBLEMS	TEACHER NOTES WITH ANSWERS

51

Numbers and Operations 1.2
Problem Solving 6.3
Representations 10.2

Draw a picture to show what $\frac{4}{3}$ means.

Answers will vary. *Possible answers:*

52

Numbers and Operations 1.1, 1.4
Algebra 2.4
Problem Solving 6.3, 6.4

The sum of two numbers is 16 and their product is 48.

What are the numbers?

4 and 12

Most students will use the guess-and-check strategy to solve this problem. Encourage them to make an organized list. This problem previews solving systems of equations in two variables.

53

Numbers and Operations 1.1
Algebra 2.1
Problem Solving 6.3
Connections 9.1

A clock strikes once at 1:00, twice at 2:00, and so on. Also, it strikes once at half past each hour.

How many times will the clock strike during one 12-hour period?

90 times

The number of times the clock strikes on the hour can be found by adding the first 12 consecutive numbers.

$$1 + 2 + 3 + 4 + 5 + 6 + 7 + 8 + 9 + 10 + 11 + 12$$

$6 \times 13 = 78$

During one 12-hour period, the clock also strikes the half hour 12 times. So, $78 + 12 = 90$.

SKILLS COVERED	**DAILY PROBLEMS**	**TEACHER NOTES WITH ANSWERS**

54

Numbers and
    Operations 1.4, 1.5
Algebra 2.3
Reasoning and Proof 7.3
Communications 8.2

Use mental computation to identify the problem that has a product of 3,286. Explain how you chose.

51×64 53×62 42×93 38×77

53×62

53×62, 51×64, and 38×77 are possibilities because their estimated products, using rounding, are between 3,000 and 3,200. The exact answer for 38×77 will be less than 3,200, however, since both factors were rounded up to get an estimate of 3,200. 51×64 cannot be a possibility because the product of the ones has 4, not 6 in the ones place. Therefore, the problem must be 53×62. Once students have made their choice, have them multiply to check.

55

Algebra 2.1
Geometry 3.1
Problem Solving 6.3

How many squares are there in this figure?

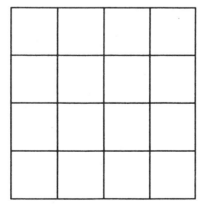

30 squares

If students answer 16 squares, guide them to see that there are other squares in the figure besides the obvious 1 by 1 squares. They can organize their counting using a table.

Size square	Number of squares
1 by 1	16
2 by 2	9
3 by 3	4
4 by 4	1
Total	30

You can extend this problem by asking students to predict the number of squares in a figure made up of 5 rows of 5 squares each. Then draw the figure and have students check their predictions. There are 30 + 25, or 55, squares in such a figure.

Answer requires writing.

	SKILLS COVERED	**DAILY PROBLEMS**	**TEACHER NOTES WITH ANSWERS**
56	**Numbers and Operations** 1.1 **Algebra** 2.1 **Reasoning and Proof** 7.2 **Representations** 10.3	The odometer on the car showed 11911, a number that is the same forward or backward. Find the next greater number that can be read the same forward or backward.	12,021 Numbers that can be read the same forward and backward are called *palindromes*. The next palindrome greater than 11,911 is 12,021.
57	**Numbers and Operations** 1.1, 1.4 **Algebra** 2.1 **Reasoning and Proof** 7.2	Find the sum of the first 10 odd numbers. Look for a shortcut.	100 The *pairing method* applied to finding the sum of the consecutive numbers in Week 2 can be applied to finding the sum of consecutive odd or even numbers. Extend this problem by asking students how they could apply the *pairing method* to finding the sum of an odd number of consecutive numbers. (Add the middle term to the total of the pairs of terms.)
58	**Numbers and Operations** 1.2 **Algebra** 2.1 **Reasoning and Proof** 7.3 **Communications** 8.1 **Representations** 10.1	Two fathers and two sons divided a pie into three equal portions. Each person ate $\frac{1}{3}$ of the pie. Explain how this is possible.	The three people dividing the pie are a grandfather, a father, and a son. The grandfather and father are the two fathers, and the father and son are the two sons.

Answer requires writing.

| SKILLS COVERED | DAILY PROBLEMS | TEACHER NOTES WITH ANSWERS |

59

Numbers and
    Operations 1.1, 1.4
Algebra 2.1
Problem Solving 6.3
Representations 10.1

Jessica has a softball game every 3 days. She has a piano lesson every 7 days. Every fourth day it is her turn to wash the dishes after supper. Today Jessica has a softball game and piano lesson, and it is her turn to wash the dishes.

How soon will these three activities occur again on the same day?

In 84 days

This problem can be solved by finding the least common multiple of 3, 4, and 7, or by making tables.

# of softball games	1	2	3	4	5	6	7	8	. . .
# of days	3	6	9	12	15	18	21	24	

# of piano lessons	1	2	3	4	5	6	7	8	. . .
# of days	7	14	21	28	35	42	49	56	

Times to wash dishes	1	2	3	4	5	6	7	8	. . .
# of days	4	8	12	16	20	24	28	32	

60

Geometry 3.1, 3.3
Problem Solving 6.3
Reasoning and Proof 7.2

Which three circles would you move to make the figure on the left look like the figure on the right?

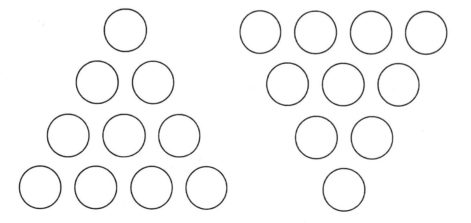

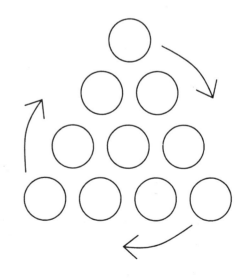

You may wish to use the standardized-test format found at the back of this manual as a review or testing option.

	SKILLS COVERED	DAILY PROBLEMS	TEACHER NOTES WITH ANSWERS
61	**Numbers and Operations** 1.3 **Measurement** 4.1 **Reasoning and Proof** 7.1 **Connections** 9.1	At Happy Foods Groceries you can buy a 5-lb package of ground beef for $11.50. At Riser Groceries a 3-lb package of the same quality ground beef sells for $6.75. Which is the better buy?	The 3-lb package for $6.75 Encourage students to use mental computation to determine the prices per pound. The 5-lb package is $0.05 per pound more expensive.

62	**Numbers and Operations** 1.1 **Geometry** 3.1 **Measurement** 4.1 **Problem Solving** 6.3, 6.4	The area of a rectangular dog pen is 48 square feet. The length of each side is a whole number. What is the least perimeter the pen could have?	28 ft Since the pen has an area of 48 square feet, the lengths of the sides must be numbers whose product is 48. Students could organize information about possible pen sizes in a table.

Length	Width	Perimeter
1 ft	48 ft	98 ft
2 ft	24 ft	52 ft
3 ft	16 ft	38 ft
4 ft	12 ft	32 ft
6 ft	8 ft	28 ft

63	**Numbers and Operations** 1.2, 1.5 **Measurement** 4.2 **Reasoning and Proof** 7.1 **Communications** 8.1	A recipe calls for $\frac{1}{3}$ cup flour. You have a $\frac{1}{4}$-cup and a $\frac{1}{2}$-cup measuring cup. How could you measure about $\frac{1}{3}$ cup of flour?	Answers will vary. *Possible answers:* Since $\frac{1}{3}$ is between $\frac{1}{4}$ and $\frac{1}{2}$, put $\frac{1}{4}$ cup and $\frac{1}{2}$ cup of flour in a bowl and take out half of it. Or you can use a little more than $\frac{1}{4}$ cup of flour, or a little less than $\frac{1}{2}$ cup. All procedures will require students to estimate.

✎ Answer requires writing.

SKILLS COVERED	DAILY PROBLEMS	TEACHER NOTES WITH ANSWERS

64

Algebra 2.1
Data Analysis 5.1
Problem Solving 6.2
Reasoning and Proof 7.2

Derek, Shana, Curt, and Lela are brothers and sisters. Each plays one of the following instruments: piano, drums, clarinet, and trumpet. Derek's brother does not use his mouth when playing his instrument. One of Derek's sisters plays the clarinet. Lela is glad she will never have to march in a parade playing her instrument.

Which instrument does each person play?

Derek: trumpet; Shana: clarinet; Curt: drums; Lela: piano

You may want to discuss with students how each sentence in the problem helps to narrow the choices of instrument each person might play. ("Lela is glad she will never have to march in a parade playing her instrument" indicates that Lela plays the piano. "One of Derek's sisters plays the clarinet" indicates that Shana or Lela plays the clarinet. Since Lela plays the piano, Shana must play the clarinet. "Derek's brother does not use his mouth when playing his instrument" indicates that Curt plays the drums or the piano. Since Lela plays the piano, Curt plays the drums. Derek must play the only instrument left, the trumpet.)

65

Numbers and Operations 1.1, 1.4
Algebra 2.1, 2.2
Problem Solving 6.3

Arrange the numbers 1–4 and 6–9 in this square so that all rows, columns, and diagonals have the same sum.

What is the magic sum?

	5	

One possible answer shown. The magic sum is 15.

8	1	6
3	5	7
4	9	2

Students may find it helpful to write each of the numbers from 1 through 9 on a separate sheet of paper and move these around as they try to solve this puzzle. They may notice that the magic sum is 3 times the number in the middle square.

SKILLS COVERED	DAILY PROBLEMS	TEACHER NOTES WITH ANSWERS

66

Numbers and Operations 1.1, 1.4
Algebra 2.4
Problem Solving 6.4
Reasoning and Proof 7.2

Find the missing digits in this problem.

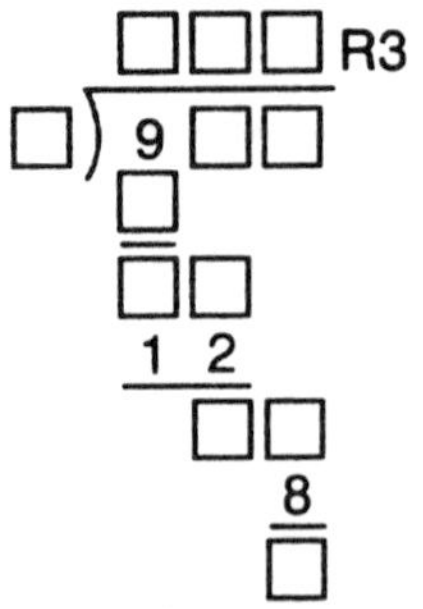

$$\begin{array}{r} \square\square\square\text{ R3} \\ \square\overline{)9\square\square} \\ \square \\ \square\square \\ 1\;2 \\ \square\square \\ 8 \\ \square \end{array}$$

$$\begin{array}{r} 232\text{ R3} \\ 4\overline{)931} \\ \underline{8} \\ 13 \\ \underline{12} \\ 11 \\ \underline{8} \\ 3 \end{array}$$

The most efficient way of solving this problem is to work backward from the remainder and use number sense.

67

Measurement 4.1
Reasoning and Proof 7.3
Communications 8.1
Connections 9.1
Representations 10.1

Jason skied down a hill in the field behind his house and made a trail 300 feet long. He climbed back up the hill along his trail. During each minute of his climb, he skied forward 10 feet, rested and slid back 4 feet.

At this rate, how long would it take Jason to reach the top of the hill? Explain your answer.

Between 49 and 50 minutes

During each whole minute, Jason's total progress up the hill is 6 feet. So, at the end of 49 minutes he will have gone 294 feet up the hill. Sometime before the end of the 50th minute, he will go forward 10 feet, putting himself over the top of the hill and, therefore, not sliding back down when he stops.

68

Numbers and Operations 1.1
Algebra 2.1, 2.3
Problem Solving 6.3
Representations 10.1

For dessert you can choose apple, cherry, blueberry, or peach pie, and milk or juice to drink.

How many different combinations can you choose from?

8 combinations

There are 4 types of pie and 2 dif[ferent drinks you] can have with each pie. Therefor[e, there are 8] combinations to choose from. So[lving this problem is aided by] seeing a tree diagram.

apple pie   cherry pie
  /\   /\
milk juice   milk juice   milk juice   milk juice

[handwritten note:]
68 M
70 T
72 W
74 T
76 F
work all

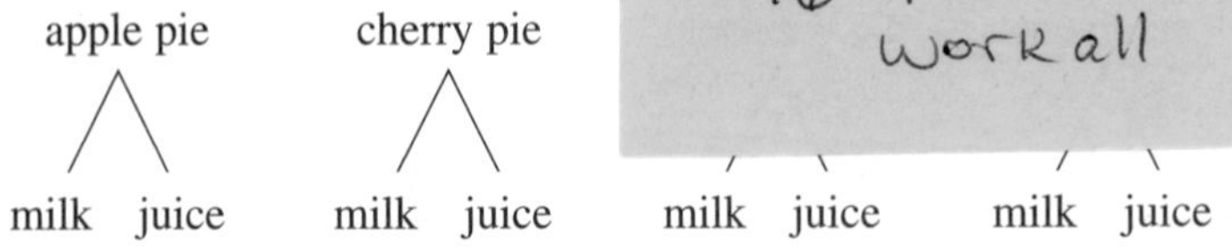

DAILYMathematics

SKILLS COVERED	DAILY PROBLEMS	TEACHER NOTES WITH ANSWERS

69 **Numbers and Operations** 1.1
Algebra 2.1
Reasoning and Proof 7.2
Representations 10.3

Solve each problem using your calculator. Look for a pattern.

$15{,}873 \times 7$

$15{,}873 \times 14$

$15{,}873 \times 21$

What is the product of $15{,}873 \times 56$? Use a calculator to check.

$15{,}873 \times 7 = 111{,}111$
$15{,}873 \times 14 = 222{,}222$
$15{,}873 \times 21 = 333{,}333$
Following the pattern of the products, $15{,}873 \times 56 = 888{,}888$.

70 **Geometry** 3.1
Measurement 4.1
Representations 10.1

If the area of each small square is 10 square centimeters, what is the area of the entire figure?

120 square centimeters

Each small square represents $\frac{1}{12}$ of the entire figure, so the area of the figure is 12×10, or 120 square centimeters.

	SKILLS COVERED	DAILY PROBLEMS	TEACHER NOTES WITH ANSWERS
71	**Numbers and Operations** 1.2 **Connections** 9.2 **Representations** 10.1, 10.3	What fraction of the letters in the word *multiply* are also in the word *product?*	$\dfrac{3}{8}$ There are 8 letters in *multiply*, so 8 is the denominator. Three letters, *u, t,* and *p,* are in both words. So, 3 is the numerator.
72	**Numbers and Operations** 1.1, 1.4 **Measurement** 4.1 **Connections** 9.1 **Representations** 10.1	At 6:00 P.M. the temperature was 14°F. By midnight, the temperature had fallen to ⁻4°F. How many degrees did the temperature fall?	18° From 14°F to 0°F is a drop of 14°. From 0°F to ⁻4°F is a drop of 4° more. Therefore, the temperature fell 14° + 4°, or 18°.
73	**Numbers and Operations** 1.1, 1.4 **Algebra** 2.1 **Reasoning and Proof** 7.3 **Communications** 8.1	Write the next number. Explain. **1.** 12, 10, 15, 13, 18, 16, 21, _____ **2.** 1, 2, 4, 5, 10, 11, 22, 23, _____	**1.** 19; Subtract 2, add 5. **2.** 46; Add 1, multiply by 2.

SKILLS COVERED	DAILY PROBLEMS	TEACHER NOTES WITH ANSWERS

74

Geometry 3.1
Problem Solving 6.3
Communications 8.1, 8.2
Representations 10.2

Lines *a*, *b*, and *c* are in the same plane.
Line *a* is perpendicular to line *b*.
Line *a* is parallel to line *c*.

How are line *b* and line *c* related?

Line *b* and line *c* are perpendicular.

Encourage students to make a sketch to determine this relationship.

You may want to extend this problem by asking students why it is necessary to state that the three lines are in the same plane. (It would be possible for lines *b* and *c* to be *skew* lines—noncoplanar and nonintersecting lines.)

75

Numbers and
   Operations 1.2
Problem Solving 6.2
Communications 8.1
Connections 9.1

Carlos is saving to buy a bike that costs $200. He has already saved one fourth of the money.

If he saves $3 per week, will he be able to buy the bike within one year? How do you know?

Yes

You may need to remind students that one fourth of $200 is $50, and that there are 52 weeks in a year. This problem can be extended by asking students to find how many weeks Carlos must save to have enough for the bike. (50)

	SKILLS COVERED	DAILY PROBLEMS	TEACHER NOTES WITH ANSWERS
76	**Algebra** 2.1 **Data Analysis** 5.3 **Reasoning and Proof** 7.3	If you toss a penny, how do you think the coin will land, heads or tails? Explain.	Students can answer heads or tails correctly. Each outcome is equally likely. Actually toss a penny numerous times and record the number of heads and tails. Although the terminology does not need to be introduced at this level, guide students in a discussion of experimental probability versus theoretical probability.
77	**Numbers and** **Operations** 1.1, 1.4 **Algebra** 2.4 **Problem Solving** 6.4 **Representations** 10.1	The total cost of a model plane and a model boat is $15. The total cost of 3 model planes and 2 model boats is $37. What is the cost of **1.** a model plane? **2.** a model boat?	**1.** $7 **2.** $8 Encourage students to use the guess-and-check strategy. This problem previews solving a system of two equations in two variables.
78	**Reasoning and** **Proof** 7.2, 7.3 **Connections** 9.2	What does this statement mean? Explain. "If you paid too much for running shoes, you didn't buy them at Sneakers City!"	It means that, if you bought the running shoes at Sneakers City, then you did not pay "too much." The statement does not say that you paid "too much" if you bought the running shoes anywhere else, but there is an attempt to imply this. However, since "too much" is so vague, this statement really says little if anything at all. Caution students to be skeptical of claims in advertisements.

✎ Answer requires writing.

SKILLS COVERED	DAILY PROBLEMS	TEACHER NOTES WITH ANSWERS

79

Algebra 2.1
Problem Solving 6.3
Connections 9.2
Representations 10.1

There are 8 teams. Suppose you set up a single-elimination tournament to determine a winner.

1. How many games will it take before a winner is determined?

2. How many games would the winning team play?

3. How many games would it take to determine a winner if there were 16 teams?

1. 7 games   **2.** 3 games   **3.** 15 games

A single-elimination tournament with 8 teams is set up as follows:

Seven games are played in all, with the two finalists each playing 3 games. A 16-team tournament would require another round for a total of 15 games.

80

Geometry 3.1, 3.2
Measurement 4.1
Problem Solving 6.3

This map shows the streets in downtown Centerville.

If traffic is only allowed to go north or east on these streets, how many different routes could a person follow to drive from the library to the park?

↑ North

10 routes

Library to *D* to *H* to *I* to *J* to Park
Library to *D* to *E* to *I* to *J* to Park
Library to *D* to *E* to *F* to *J* to Park
Library to *D* to *E* to *F* to *G* to Park
Library to *A* to *E* to *I* to *J* to Park
Library to *A* to *E* to *F* to *J* to Park
Library to *A* to *E* to *F* to *G* to Park
Library to *A* to *B* to *F* to *J* to Park
Library to *A* to *B* to *F* to *G* to Park
Library to *A* to *B* to *C* to *G* to Park

You may wish to use the standardized-test format found at the back of this manual as a review or testing option.

SKILLS COVERED	DAILY PROBLEMS	TEACHER NOTES WITH ANSWERS
81 **Numbers and** **Operations** 1.3, 1.4 **Algebra** 2.3 **Representations** 10.3	What mathematical symbol would you need to place between 2 and 3 so that the result is a number between 2 and 3?	A decimal point: 2.3 You can extend this problem by asking students to name numbers between 2 and 3. Since the Density Property states that between any two rational numbers there is another rational number, students will give many different examples. (2.31, 2.5, 2.7, 2.999, etc.)
82 **Numbers and** **Operations** 1.1 **Algebra** 2.1 **Reasoning and Proof** 7.2	Find each quotient. Look for a pattern. $21 \div 3 =$ $201 \div 3 =$ $2,001 \div 3 =$ Use the pattern you found. What is the quotient of $200,001 \div 3$?	$21 \div 3 = 7$ $201 \div 3 = 67$ $2,001 \div 3 = 667$ Following the pattern established in the quotients above, $200,001 \div 3 = 66,667$. Students can verify this using a calculator.
83 **Numbers and** **Operations** 1.2 **Measurement** 4.1 **Reasoning and Proof** 7.1 **Connections** 9.1	Maria ran 450 yards. Brittany ran $\frac{1}{4}$ mile. Who ran farther? How much farther?	Maria ran 10 yards farther. To solve this problem, students need to know that there are 1,760 yards in a mile. If they have forgotten this, have them use the fact that there are 5,280 feet in a mile to derive the number of yards in a mile.

SKILLS COVERED	DAILY PROBLEMS	TEACHER NOTES WITH ANSWERS

84

Algebra 2.1
Data Analysis 5.3
Reasoning and Proof 7.3
Communications 8.1

You have 8 white socks and 8 blue socks in your drawer.
You reach in without looking and pull out one sock at a time.

What is the fewest number of socks you would need to take out to be sure you got a matching pair? Explain.

You would need to pull out 3 socks at most. If the first 2 socks are a white and a blue sock, the third sock will either be white or blue and will match one of the first two.

Extend this problem by discussing whether the number of socks that must be pulled out would change if the number of colors of socks changed. (Yes; for example, if there were three different colors of socks, as many as 4 socks may have to be pulled out to get a matching pair.)

85

Geometry 3.1
Problem Solving 6.3
Reasoning and Proof 7.2
Representations 10.1

Here are two ways that a square can be divided into four equal parts.

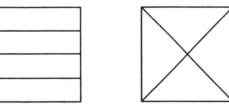

Find two other ways in which this can be done.

Possible answers include:

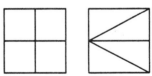

	SKILLS COVERED	DAILY PROBLEMS	TEACHER NOTES WITH ANSWERS
86	**Numbers and Operations** 1.1 **Algebra** 2.4 **Problem Solving** 6.1, 6.2, 6.4	The combined ages of Joel, his father, and his grandfather are equal to 100. Joel is 25 years younger than his father and 51 years younger than his grandfather. How old are Joel, his father, and his grandfather?	8; 33; 59 Many students may use guess-and-check as their problem-solving strategy. However, another way to approach this problem is to add 25 and 51, the father's and grandfather's ages when Joel was born (76). $100 - 76 = 24$ and $24 \div 3 = 8$. Joel would have to be 8, his father $25 + 8$, and his grandfather $51 + 8$.
87	**Numbers and Operations** 1.3, 1.5 **Measurement** 4.2 **Reasoning and Proof** 7.1 **Communications** 8.2	Which is the better buy, a gallon of paint for $11.75 or a quart of paint for $3.25?	A gallon for $11.75 You may need to remind students that there are 4 quarts in a gallon. Encourage them to use mental math or estimation to determine that a gallon for $11.75 is the better buy.
88	**Numbers and Operations** 1.1 **Measurement** 4.1, 4.2 **Reasoning and Proof** 7.1 **Connections** 9.1	The Wabash Cannonball traveled 55 miles in 50 minutes. The Orange Blossom Special covered 136 miles in 2 hours. Which train had the greater average speed?	The Orange Blossom Special Encourage students to use number sense to solve this problem. The Orange Blossom Special can travel 68 miles in one hour ($136 \div 2$). The Wabash Cannonball can travel 11 miles ($55 \div 5$) every 10 minutes ($50 \div 5$), or 66 miles in one hour. This problem previews the concept of proportions.

| **SKILLS COVERED** | **DAILY PROBLEMS** | **TEACHER NOTES WITH ANSWERS** |

89

Numbers and Operations 1.5
Algebra 2.3
Reasoning and Proof 7.3
Communications 8.1, 8.2

1. Which number is the easiest to mentally add to 76: 35, 37, or 39? Explain why you think so.

2. Which number is easiest to mentally subtract from 274: 32, 35, or 37? Explain.

Answers will vary. Possible answers:

1. 39; Add 40 to 76 and subtract 1.

2. 32; Subtracting 32 from 274 requires no regrouping.

Accept any choice that students can justify.

90

Geometry 3.1, 3.3
Problem Solving 6.3
Reasoning and Proof 7.2

How can you move just three toothpicks and form three small squares?

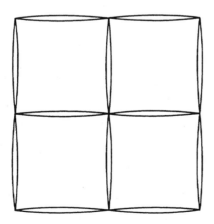

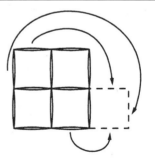
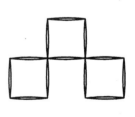

You may want to have students use toothpicks to solve this problem.

SKILLS COVERED	DAILY PROBLEMS	TEACHER NOTES WITH ANSWERS

91

Numbers and Operations 1.1
Problem Solving 6.1
Reasoning and Proof 7.2
Communications 8.1
Representations 10.1

Mark has 2 quarters, 3 nickels, and 3 pennies.
Juanita has 1 quarter, 2 dimes, and 1 penny.
Frank has 1 half-dollar and 4 pennies.

How can Mark, Juanita, and Frank share the coins so that each has the same amount of money?

How did you find your answer?

Answers will vary. *Possible answer:* Mark can give 2 nickels to Juanita and 2 pennies to Frank.

The total value of the coins is $1.68, so for each person to have the same amount of money, each must have 168 ÷ 3, or 56, cents. Any combination of coins that achieves this result is acceptable.

92

Numbers and Operations 1.1, 1.4
Algebra 2.4
Problem Solving 6.1
Reasoning and Proof 7.2

Insert one operation sign to make each number sentence correct.

1. 4 0 4 4 = 101

2. 2 3 5 6 = 712

3. 4 2 7 9 = 418

4. 6 7 8 9 = 156

1. $404 \div 4 = 101$
2. $2 \times 356 = 712$
3. $427 - 9 = 418$
4. $67 + 89 = 156$

Guide students who are having difficulty with these number sentences to look at the numbers possible on the left side of the equals sign. For example, in the first number sentence a relation between 4 and 101 or 40 and 101 is not evident. However, a relation between 404 and 101 is.

93

Numbers and Operations 1.4
Algebra 2.3
Reasoning and Proof 7.2
Representations 10.3

What is the greatest 6-digit number in which the digit in the thousands place is twice the digit in the tens place?

What is the least number?

998,949; 100,000

You may want to point out that no restrictions are given on using a digit more than once.

Answer requires writing.

SKILLS COVERED	DAILY PROBLEMS	TEACHER NOTES WITH ANSWERS

94

Numbers and Operations 1.2
Algebra 2.1
Data Analysis 5.1
Problem Solving 6.3
Reasoning and Proof 7.2

In the Ortez family, there is a grandmother and a grandfather. There are also 4 mothers and 2 fathers. Half of the mothers have 3 daughters and half have 1 daughter. Half of the fathers have 2 sons and half have 1 son.

What is the fewest number of people there could be in the Ortez family?

13 people

You may need to point out that it is possible for one person to be a different relation to different people. A diagram may help students organize their thinking.

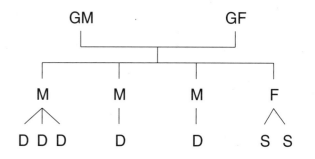

95

Geometry 3.1, 3.3
Problem Solving 6.3
Reasoning and Proof 7.2

How can you cut this 3 by 10 rectangle into two pieces and place them together to form a 2 by 15 rectangle?

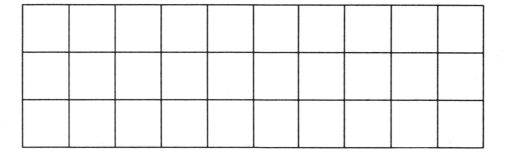

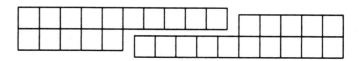

Students may need to draw the rectangle on grid paper, cut it apart, and move pieces around until they form a 2 by 15 rectangle.

	SKILLS COVERED	DAILY PROBLEMS	TEACHER NOTES WITH ANSWERS

96

Algebra 2.4
Data Analysis 5.2
Problem Solving 6.1
Representations 10.1

The range of a baseball team's scores for four games is 9.
The scores for three games are 5, 3, and 8.

What is the score for the fourth game?
Explain how you find it.

12

The *range* of a set of data is the difference between the highest and the lowest values. The range of game scores is 9, but the difference between any two given scores is not 9. Therefore, the given scores include the highest or lowest score, but not both. The given scores cannot contain the highest value, because the highest score given is 8, and $8 - 9$ is less than zero. Therefore, the given scores must include the lowest score, or 3. Since $3 + 9 = 12$, the other score is 12.

97

Numbers and Operations 1.1
Algebra 2.1, 2.2
Representations 10.3

Complete each problem. Look for a pattern.

$1 \times 9 + 2 =$

$12 \times 9 + 3 =$

$123 \times 9 + 4 =$

Use the pattern you discovered to find the missing number.

_____ $\times 9 + 8 = 11,111,111$

$1 \times 9 + 2 = 11$
$12 \times 9 + 3 = 111$
$123 \times 9 + 4 = 1,111$

Missing number: 1,234,567

The first number in each problem has one fewer digit than the answer and consists of the counting numbers in consecutive order. Since 11,111,111 has 8 digits, the missing number will consist of the first 7 counting numbers—1,234,567. You may need to remind students that by the order of operations, multiplication is performed before addition.

98

Numbers and Operations 1.1
Problem Solving 6.2
Connections 9.2
Representations 10.1

Abraham Lincoln's Gettysburg Address begins,

   "Four score and seven years ago our fathers brought forth
     on this continent a new nation . . ."

1. How many years is four score and seven years?

2. Lincoln delivered this speech in 1863. What year was he referring to in his opening words?

1. 87
2. 1776

If students do not know how many years are in a score, tell them that a score of years ago was [name the year 20 years earlier].

✎ Answer requires writing.

SKILLS COVERED	DAILY PROBLEMS	TEACHER NOTES WITH ANSWERS

99

Numbers and Operations 1.1
Algebra 2.1, 2.3
Problem Solving 6.3
Representations 10.1

On their vacation the Chins plan to visit a museum, a beach, and an amusement park. They have their choice of a science, a history, or an art museum; a beach on the ocean or at a lake; and a water-ride park or a park with a giant roller coaster.

In how many different ways can the Chins visit a museum, then a beach, and finally an amusement park?

12 ways

Making a tree diagram or an organized list would be an effective strategy for finding the 12 possible ways.

science museum
— ocean beach
 — water park—science, ocean, water
 — coaster park—science, ocean, coaster
— lake beach
 — water park—science, lake, water
 — coaster park—science, lake, coaster

history museum
— ocean beach
 — water park—history, ocean, water
 — coaster park—history, ocean, coaster
— lake beach
 — water park—history, lake, water
 — coaster park—history, lake, coaster

art museum
— ocean beach
 — water park—art, ocean, water
 — coaster park—art, ocean, coaster
— lake beach
 — water park—art, lake, water
 — coaster park—art, lake, coaster

100

Geometry 3.1, 3.3
Problem Solving 6.3
Reasoning and Proof 7.2

Rearrange the circles in the diagram to form rows of 4.

You may want to have students use 9 pennies to help solve the problem. Any other answer that students can justify is acceptable.

SKILLS COVERED	DAILY PROBLEMS	TEACHER NOTES WITH ANSWERS
101 **Geometry** 3.1 **Measurement** 4.1 **Problem Solving** 6.2, 6.3 **Representations** 10.1	What is the surface area of a cube whose sides have lengths of 5 inches?	150 square inches You may need to point out that surface area is the sum of the areas of all the surfaces of an object, even the bottom. This cube has 6 square surfaces, each 5 inches by 5 inches. Since the area of each surface is 5×5, or 25, square inches, the surface area of the entire cube is 6×25, or 150, square inches.
102 **Algebra** 2.2, 2.3, 2.4 **Representations** 10.3	Using the same 1-digit number three times in an expression, write two expressions that are equal to 20.	$4 \times 4 + 4 = 20$; $5 \times 5 - 5 = 20$ Challenge the students to find other numbers that can be written as an expression made up of the same three 1-digit numbers.
103 **Numbers and Operations** 1.3, 1.5 **Problem Solving** 6.2 **Communications** 8.1	Which is the less expensive way of ordering 80 packets? **Mail-Order Catalog** 10 packets . . . . . . $7.50 100 packets $49.50	Order 100 packets for $49.50 If you order eight 10-packets, you will pay $8 \times$ $7.50, or $60.00. You would save $10.50 by ordering 100 packets for $49.50.

SKILLS COVERED	DAILY PROBLEMS	TEACHER NOTES WITH ANSWERS

104 **Numbers and Operations** 1.2
Algebra 2.3
Communications 8.1, 8.2
Representations 10.3

What is the least fraction you can write using the digits 3, 4, and 5 each only once? What is the greatest? Explain your answers.

$\dfrac{3}{54}, \dfrac{54}{3}$

The greater the denominator, the lesser the fractional parts.

The lesser the denominator, the greater the fractional parts.

For example, $\dfrac{3}{54}$ must be less than $\dfrac{4}{53}$ since 54ths are less than 53rds, and 3 of the lesser parts must be less than 4 of the greater parts. Also, $\dfrac{54}{3}$ must be greater than $\dfrac{53}{4}$ since 3rds are greater than 4ths, and 54 of the greater parts must be greater than 53 of the lesser parts.

105 **Numbers and Operations** 1.1, 1.4
Algebra 2.1
Problem Solving 6.2
Reasoning and Proof 7.2

Fill in the circles using each of the numbers 1, 2, 3, 4, 6, 9, and 18 once. The product of the three numbers on each line must be equal to 72.

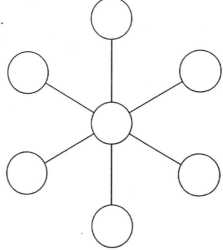

Encourage students to use the guess-and-check strategy to identify pairs of numbers which have the same product.

	SKILLS COVERED	**DAILY PROBLEMS**	**TEACHER NOTES WITH ANSWERS**

106   **Measurement** 4.1, 4.2
Problem Solving 6.2
Reasoning and Proof 7.1, 7.3
Communications 8.1

Daniel is 5 times as old as his sister Rachel. In 2 years he will be 3 times as old. After 4 more years, he will be only twice as old.

When will they be the same age?

They will never be the same age.

The relationship between Daniel's age and Rachel's age seems to be approaching the point when they will be the same. However, students can use the guess-and-check strategy to find that Daniel is currently 10 and Rachel is 2.

---

107   **Geometry** 3.1, 3.3
Problem Solving 6.3
Representations 10.1

There are rectangular tables in the school cafeteria. Two students can sit on each side, and one student can sit at each end.

How many tables need to be pushed together to form one long table that will seat 34? Explain.

8 tables

Only 2 out of 34 students can sit at the ends of the long rectangular table, one at each end. The remaining 32 students must sit along the sides, 16 students on each side. Since 2 students can sit on one side of each table, $16 \div 2$, or 8, tables are needed. Suggest that students make a diagram to help them visualize the problem.

---

108   **Numbers and Operations** 1.2
Measurement 4.2
Reasoning and Proof 7.2
Communications 8.1

Ashley brought $\frac{3}{8}$ pound of pecans and $\frac{5}{8}$ pound of walnuts.

She stated that she bought $\frac{1}{2}$ pound of nuts. Was Ashley correct?

If not, what mistake do you think she made?

What total amount of nuts did she buy?

No. She may have added the fractions by adding the numerators and the denominators. She bought $\frac{8}{8}$ pound, or 1 pound.

Extend this problem by asking students how they could tell that Ashley's answer was incorrect without working out the problem. ($\frac{5}{8}$, the weight of one part of nuts, is greater than $\frac{1}{2}$, the total Ashley found.)

✎ Answer requires writing.

SKILLS COVERED	DAILY PROBLEMS	TEACHER NOTES WITH ANSWERS

109   **Numbers and Operations** 1.1, 1.4
Algebra 2.4
Reasoning and Proof 7.2

1. Insert one operation sign into a row of 5 ones to get 100.

2. Insert one operation sign into a row of 6 twos to get 101.

3. Insert one operation sign into a row of 4 threes to get 111.

1. $111 - 11 = 100$
2. $2{,}222 \div 22 = 101$
3. $333 \div 3 = 111$

You may wish to have students make up their own similar problems.

---

110   **Algebra** 2.1, 2.3
Problem Solving 6.1
Reasoning and Proof 7.3
Representations 10.2

1. Apply the rule of the function machine to each number in the table.

In	1	2	3	4	5	6
Out	3					

2. What rule did the function machine apply to the table?

In	1	2	3	4	5	6
Out	1	4	9	16	25	36

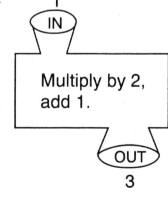

1

IN

Multiply by 2, add 1.

OUT

3

1.

In	1	2	3	4	5	6
Out	3	5	7	9	11	13

2. Answers may vary. *Possible answers:* Multiply the number by itself; square the number

This problem previews the algebraic concept of *functions*. You may want to stress that for each number that is put into the machine (input), exactly one number comes out (output).

SKILLS COVERED	DAILY PROBLEMS	TEACHER NOTES WITH ANSWERS
111 **Numbers and Operations** 1.1 **Measurement** 4.1 **Representations** 10.1	A fathom is a unit of measure equivalent to 6 feet. How many fathoms are in a mile?	880 fathoms If students have forgotten how many feet are in a mile, remind them that there are 1,760 yards in a mile and let them derive the number of feet from this.
112 **Numbers and Operations** 1.4 **Algebra** 2.3 **Communications** 8.1, 8.2 **Representations** 10.3	These numbers are written in order, from least to greatest. 43☐,258 43☐,750 43☐,425 Could all three missing digits be the same? Explain.	No The missing digit in the first and second numbers could be the same, but the missing digit in the third number would have to be greater since the hundreds digit in the third number is less than in the second.

113 **Numbers and Operations** 1.3, 1.4
 Algebra 2.2
 Problem Solving 6.4
 Reasoning and Proof 7.2
	Find the missing digits in this problem.
	
	     ☐ 7 . 4 ☐
	    + ☐ . 8 1
	     ‾‾‾‾‾‾‾‾‾‾
	     3 6 . 3 ☐
		27.49
		 + 8.81
		 ‾‾‾‾‾
		 36.30
		
		 Guide students who are having difficulty with questions such as, "Is 4 plus 8 equal to 3 or 13? If not, how is it possible to have a 3 in the tens place of the answer?" ($1 + 4 + 8 = 13$; this is possible if a 1 is regrouped from the ones column. This is possible if the problem in the ones column is $9 + 1 = 10$.)

✎ Answer requires writing.

SKILLS COVERED	DAILY PROBLEMS	TEACHER NOTES WITH ANSWERS

---

114 **Geometry** 3.1, 3.3
Problem Solving 6.3
Reasoning and Proof 7.2

Show how you could divide a circle into 11 pieces using only 4 straight lines.

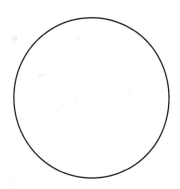

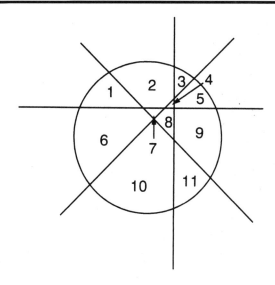

---

115 **Data Analysis** 5.2
Problem Solving 6.2, 6.4
Reasoning and Proof 7.3
Communications 8.1

What must the temperature be on Friday to have a 5-day average of 42°F? Explain how you found your answer.

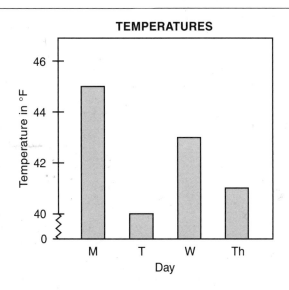

TEMPERATURES

41°

Students can work backward to solve this problem. The average of 5 numbers is found by adding the five numbers, then dividing by 5. To work backward, multiply the given average by 5, then subtract the sum of the four known daily temperatures.

Answer requires writing.

SKILLS COVERED	DAILY PROBLEMS	TEACHER NOTES WITH ANSWERS
116 **Numbers and Operations** 1.2 **Problem Solving** 6.3 **Connections** 9.1 **Representations** 10.1	On the hour, a clock chimes once for each hour. Each chime lasts 1 second, and there is a $\frac{1}{2}$-second rest between chimes. How long does it take this clock to chime for 6:00?	$8\frac{1}{2}$ seconds There will be a total of 6 seconds for the chimes and five $\frac{1}{2}$-second rests between chimes.
117 **Numbers and Operations** 1.3, 1.4 **Algebra** 2.3 **Communications** 8.1, 8.2	One of the answer choices below is correct. Without doing any computations, explain how you can tell which of the answer choices given are incorrect. $$5.58 + 3.26 =$$ 88.4 2.32 8.84 8.82	88.4 is not the correct answer because the estimated sum is $5 + 3$, or 8. 2.32 is not the correct answer because this is less than either of the numbers being added. 8.82 is not the correct answer because the first partial sum that must be found is $8 + 6$, or 14, which would not result in writing a 2 in the hundredths place. If students work the problem, they will find that the remaining answer, 8.84, is indeed correct. Encourage students to use mental computations when possible.
118 **Numbers and Operations** 1.1, 1.5 **Algebra** 2.1 **Data Analysis** 5.2 **Reasoning and Proof** 7.1, 7.2	Which averages could you find using mental math? Explain. 1. 22, 26, 24 2. 48, 47, 45 3. 53, 54, 56, 58 4. 34, 35, 37, 38	Answers will vary. *Possible answer:* Problems 1 and 4 Using number sense, students may recognize that the average in problem 1 is the middle term when the numbers are written in order, since each of the other terms are equally lesser and greater. The average in problem 4 is the number halfway between the two middle terms since the first two terms and the last two terms are equally lesser and greater than this number. Students may wish to use a calculator to check their reasoning. Any other answer that students can justify is also acceptable.

Answer requires writing.

SKILLS COVERED	DAILY PROBLEMS	TEACHER NOTES WITH ANSWERS

119   **Numbers and Operations** 1.1, 1.4
Algebra 2.1
Problem Solving 6.3
Representations 10.1

A cereal company puts a 25¢-off coupon in every other box of cereal it packages. It puts a pencil in every fifth box. It puts a coupon for a free gallon of milk in every eighth box.

Out of the first 100 boxes, how many will have a 25¢-off coupon, a pencil, and a coupon for a free gallon of milk?

2 boxes (the 40th and the 80th boxes)

Students can solve this problem by finding the least common multiple of 2, 5, and 8. The next common multiple of these three numbers greater than 40 and less than 100 is 80.

---

120   **Geometry** 3.1
Measurement 4.1, 4.2
Problem Solving 6.3

What is the area of the figure?

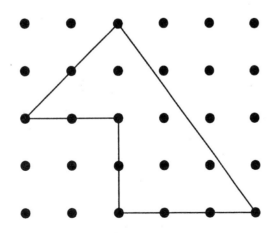

8 square units

Suggest that students divide the figure into two triangles whose areas can be added. Remind students that the area of a triangle is half the area of a rectangle with the same height and width (base).

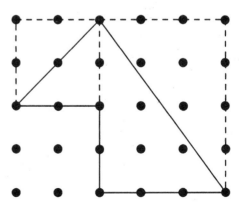

You may wish to use the standardized-test format found at the back of this manual as a review or testing option.

SKILLS COVERED	DAILY PROBLEMS	TEACHER NOTES WITH ANSWERS
121 **Algebra** 2.1 **Measurement** 4.1 **Problem Solving** 6.3 **Representations** 10.1	Ben is building a fence. He places 15 fence posts 8 feet apart. What is the distance from the first fence post to the last?	112 feet Since there are 15 fence posts, there are 14 spaces between posts. Each space is 8 feet wide, so the total distance is 14×8, or 112, feet. If students have difficulty visualizing this problem, suggest that they draw a diagram.

122 **Numbers and**
     Operations 1.3, 1.4
 Algebra 2.1, 2.3
 Reasoning and Proof 7.2
 Representations 10.3
	These decimals are written in order, from least to greatest.
	
	    0.22☐ 0.☐24 0.3☐4
	
	 The missing digit in each number is the same.
	
	 What two digits could ☐ stand for?
		2 or 3
		
		 The answer could be 0.222, 0.224, 0.324, or 0.223, 0.324, 0.334.

123 **Numbers and**
     Operations 1.1, 1.5
 Problem Solving 6.3
 Communications 8.1
 Representations 10.1
	Show how you would mentally compute $4{,}000 - 1{,}376$.	Answers will vary. *Possible answers:*
		 $4{,}000 - 1{,}000 = 3{,}000$
		 $3{,}000 - 300 = 2{,}700$
		 $2{,}700 - 70 = 2{,}630$
		 $2{,}630 - 6 = 2{,}624$
		      or
		 Subtract 1 from 4,000 to get 3,999.
		 Subtract 1 from 1,376 to get 1,375.
		 Then subtract from right to left to get 2,624.
		 Any answer that students can justify is acceptable.

SKILLS COVERED	DAILY PROBLEMS	TEACHER NOTES WITH ANSWERS

124 **Algebra** 2.1
Data Analysis 5.1
Problem Solving 6.3
Communications 8.1, 8.2

Suppose your parents give you the choice of the following two allowance plans.

    Plan A: $5 per week

    Plan B: Start with 1¢ the first week.

    Each week your allowance doubles.

Which plan would you choose? Why?

Plan B; Results in a tremendously greater allowance

A table may help students see how quickly the numbers increase by doubling.

Week	Plan A	Plan B
1	$5.00	$0.01
2	$5.00	$0.02
3	$5.00	$0.04
4	$5.00	$0.08
5	$5.00	$0.16
6	$5.00	$0.32
7	$5.00	$0.64
8	$5.00	$1.28
9	$5.00	$2.56
10	$5.00	$5.12
11	$5.00	$10.24
12	$5.00	$20.48
13	$5.00	$40.96

125 **Numbers and Operations** 1.1
Algebra 2.1, 2.4
Problem Solving 6.2
Reasoning and Proof 7.2

Arrange each of the numbers 1 through 9 in these circles so that the sum of the numbers along each side of the triangle is 17.

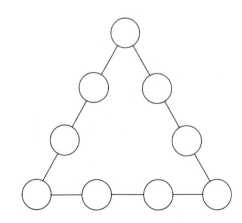

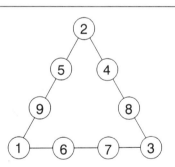

Answers will vary. One example is shown. To get students started, you may want to ask them which circles will contain numbers that are added to more than one side (the circles at the corners [or vertices]). Help students realize that using lesser numbers here would be a good idea since the sum to be reached is not a very great number.

SKILLS COVERED	DAILY PROBLEMS	TEACHER NOTES WITH ANSWERS

126 **Numbers and Operations** 1.1
Algebra 2.1
Reasoning and Proof 7.2
Representations 10.3

Solve each of these problems. Look for a pattern.

$37 \times 3 =$

$37 \times 6 =$

$37 \times 9 =$

What is the product of 37×27? Use a calculator to check.

$37 \times 3 = 111$
$37 \times 6 = 222$
$37 \times 9 = 333$

In line with the pattern established, the product of 37×27 is 999.

---

127 **Numbers and Operations** 1.1, 1.4
Algebra 2.2, 2.3, 2.4

Fill in △ and ☐ with numbers that will make the equation true.

$$\triangle + \square + \square = 9$$

7, 1, 1; 5, 2, 2; 3, 3, 3; 1, 4, 4

You may need to point out that both squares must be replaced by the same number. The triangle can be replaced with a different number or the same number that replaces the square. This problem previews the algebraic concept of variables.

---

128 **Measurement** 4.1
Problem Solving 6.2
Communications 8.1
Connections 9.1
Representations 10.1

About how many seconds do you sleep each night? Explain how you found your answer.

Answers will vary based on the number of hours students sleep. *Possible answers:* A student who sleeps for 8 hours will sleep 28,800 seconds. A student who sleeps for 10 hours will sleep 36,000 seconds.

Any reasonable answer is acceptable. If a student gives an unreasonable response, you may need to remind the student that there are 60×60, or 3,600, seconds in one hour.

Answer requires writing.

SKILLS COVERED	DAILY PROBLEMS	TEACHER NOTES WITH ANSWERS

129   **Algebra** 2.1, 2.4
Measurement 4.2
Problem Solving 6.3

At the end of the track meet Team A had 5 points less than Team B. Team D had 15 points more than Team A. Team B had 15 points more than Team C.

What was the order of finish?

D, B, A, C

You may want to discuss how each sentence of the problem helps determine the order in which the teams finished. Students may find it helpful to assign points to each team according to the description in the problem.

For example:

Team A	20 points
Team B	25 points
Team C	10 points
Team D	35 points

---

130   **Geometry** 3.1, 3.3
Problem Solving 6.3

How many squares are in this figure?

15 squares

You may need to point out that there are five different sizes of squares. Students may forget to include the largest square.

SKILLS COVERED	DAILY PROBLEMS	TEACHER NOTES WITH ANSWERS

131 **Numbers and Operations** 1.4
Algebra 2.3
Reasoning and Proof 7.1, 7.3
Communications 8.2

Without doing the computation, explain how you can determine which of the given choices are not a solution to the problem.

$$42,678 - 38,981 =$$

    3,659   3,697   13,697   81,659

3,659 cannot be the correct answer because the difference of the digits in the ones column is 7, not 9.

13,697 cannot be the correct answer because rounding to the nearest thousand results in a difference of 4,000, not 14,000.

81,659 cannot be the correct answer because it is greater than either of the numbers in the problem.

---

132 **Geometry** 3.1
Measurement 4.1
Problem Solving 6.3
Reasoning and Proof 7.1
Connections 9.1

Five flags are spaced evenly around a track. It took a runner 30 seconds to get from the first flag to the third flag.

If the runner continues at the same speed, how long will it take her to get completely around the track?

75 seconds, or 1 minute 15 seconds

Encourage students to draw a diagram of the track and flags. The diagram should show five intervals between flags. To go from the first flag to the third flag, the runner must complete two of the intervals. If a runner can do this in 30 seconds, it takes 15 seconds to complete each interval and 5 × 15, or 75 seconds to complete the entire track.

---

133 **Numbers and Operations** 1.1, 1.4
Algebra 2.1, 2.4
Reasoning and Proof 7.1

It takes 4 carpenters 4 minutes to nail 4 boards in place.

At this rate, how long will it take 80 carpenters to nail 80 boards in place?

4 minutes

You may need to point out that it takes each carpenter 4 minutes to nail 1 board in place.

✎ Answer requires writing.

SKILLS COVERED	DAILY PROBLEMS	TEACHER NOTES WITH ANSWERS

134   **Algebra** 2.1
Measurement 4.1, 4.2
Problem Solving 6.3
Representations 10.1

Armando has a pocket full of change, yet he can't make change for a dollar, a half-dollar, a quarter, a dime, or a nickel.

What is the greatest amount of money Armando can have in his pocket, assuming he does not have a dollar coin?

$1.19 (1 half-dollar, 1 quarter, 4 dimes, 4 pennies)

You may want to have students use slips of paper for coins to help solve this problem.

---

135   **Geometry** 3.1, 3.3
Problem Solving 6.3
Reasoning and Proof 7.2

How can the 9 toothpicks be rearranged to form 5 equilateral triangles?

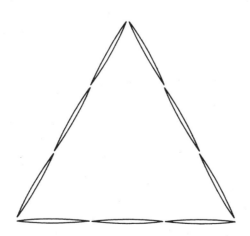

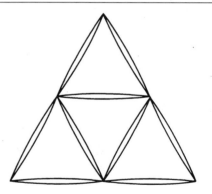

You may need to remind students that all sides of an equilateral triangle have the same length. You may also want to have students use toothpicks to help solve this problem.

SKILLS COVERED	DAILY PROBLEMS	TEACHER NOTES WITH ANSWERS
136 **Numbers and Operations** 1.1, 1.4 **Algebra** 2.1, 2.4 **Geometry** 3.1 **Measurement** 4.1	A rectangle has a perimeter of 30 cm. The length and width are each whole numbers. What is the greatest possible area the rectangle could have?	56 square centimeters Since the perimeter is 30 cm, the sum of the rectangle's length and width is 15 cm. Students need to find the pair of addends whose sum is 15 that yields the greatest product. (7 and 8)
137 **Numbers and Operations** 1.1, 1.4 **Algebra** 2.3, 2.4 **Communications** 8.1, 8.2	Without doing any computations, tell how many digits (not counting any remainder) are in each of the following quotients. Explain how you decided. 1. 567 ÷ 7 2. 90,354 ÷ 5 3. 23,168 ÷ 14 4. 496,112 ÷ 88	**1.** 2 digits **2.** 5 digits **3.** 4 digits **4.** 4 digits You may need to remind students that the remainder is not part of the quotient. Suggest that students who are having difficulty rewrite each problem using)‾ . Have them identify the digit of the dividend that the first digit of the quotient will be written above. Then have them count this digit plus the remaining digits in the quotient.
138 **Connections** 9.1 **Representations** 10.1	Where does 8 plus 5 make 1?	On a clock (8:00 plus 5 hours is 1:00.)

✎ Answer requires writing.

SKILLS COVERED	DAILY PROBLEMS	TEACHER NOTES WITH ANSWERS

139   **Numbers and Operations** 1.2, 1.3, 1.4
Algebra 2.3
Reasoning and Proof 7.1
Representations 10.3

Arrange these numbers in order, from least to greatest.

0.5 $\dfrac{3}{5}$ 0.45 $\dfrac{4}{20}$

$\dfrac{4}{20}$, 0.45, 0.5, $\dfrac{3}{5}$

You may want to suggest that students rewrite all the numbers as fractions with the same denominator (100), or as decimals.

---

140   **Geometry** 3.1, 3.2
Problem Solving 6.3
Representations 10.1, 10.2

When the Changs left the museum to return to their hotel, they walked 5 blocks north, 4 blocks east, 3 blocks south, and 1 block west. Then they realized they were lost.

1. How far were they from their hotel?

2. What is the most direct route they could have taken to get from the museum to their hotel?

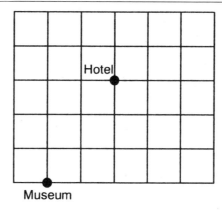

1. 2 blocks (1 block south and 1 block east)
2. 3 blocks north and 2 blocks east, in any order

You may wish to use the standardized-test format found at the back of this manual as a review or testing option.

SKILLS COVERED	DAILY PROBLEMS	TEACHER NOTES WITH ANSWERS

141   **Algebra** 2.1
Data Analysis 5.3
Reasoning and Proof 7.3
Communications 8.1

What is the chance of getting an even number when you toss a number cube 10 times? Explain your answer.

$\frac{5}{10}$, or $\frac{1}{2}$; because three of the numbers are even and three are odd, there is an equal chance of rolling either.

You may want to have students conduct this experiment in class. Help students conclude that the results of the experimental probability are close to the theoretical probability. You may want to conduct the experiment several times, increasing the number of times the cube is tossed to 20, 30, or 40.

---

142   **Numbers and Operations** 1.4
Algebra 2.2, 2.3, 2.4
Problem Solving 6.4
Representations 10.2

Replace the $\triangle$ and the $\square$ with numbers that make both equations true at the same time.

$$\triangle \times \square = 24$$

$$\triangle \times \triangle = 36$$

$\triangle = 6;\ \square = 4$

Encourage students to use the guess-and-check strategy to solve this problem. You may need to point out that each triangle in the equations must be replaced by the same number. This problem previews solving systems of equations in two variables.

---

143   **Geometry** 3.1, 3.3
Problem Solving 6.3
Communications 8.1
Connections 9.1

You have 4 red checkers and 4 black checkers.

How can you arrange all these checkers to form 6 straight lines with exactly 2 red checkers in each and 2 straight lines with exactly 2 black checkers in each?

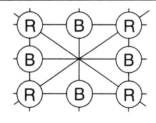

You may wish to make checkers or two different-colored counters available to students, or encourage them to use pieces of paper labeled "red" and "black."

✎ Answer requires writing.

| **SKILLS COVERED** | **DAILY PROBLEMS** | **TEACHER NOTES WITH ANSWERS** |

144 **Numbers and Operations**
1.1, 1.3, 1.4, 1.5
Algebra 2.3
Reasoning and Proof 7.1

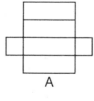 Identify the problems that have unreasonable answers. Explain why these answers are unreasonable.

1. $3.46 \times 4 = 138.4$

2. $5,282 \div 38 = 139$

3. $48.2 \times 5 = 28.92$

4. $4,136 \div 52 = 709 \text{ R}28$

1. 3.46 can be rounded to 3; $3 \times 4 = 12$.

3. When multiplying by numbers greater than 1, the product is greater than either of the factors. In this problem, the product is less than the first factor.

4. 52 will not divide 41, but it will divide 413. Therefore, the quotient will be a 2-digit, not a 3-digit number.

145 **Geometry** 3.1, 3.3
Problem Solving 6.3
Representations 10.2

Which nets can be folded to form rectangular prisms?

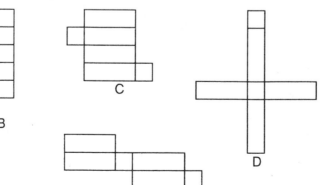

A, C, D, F

If students are having difficulty visualizing which nets can be folded to form rectangular prisms, have them sketch each net, cut it out, and try to make a rectangular prism.

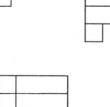

	SKILLS COVERED	**DAILY PROBLEMS**	**TEACHER NOTES WITH ANSWERS**

---

146 **Numbers and Operations** 1.3, 1.5
Measurement 4.1
Problem Solving 6.1, 6.2
Connections 9.1

A grocery store sells three different-size cans of a certain brand of tomato paste, as shown in the chart.

Size	Price
8 oz	$0.48
15 oz	$0.85
22 oz	$1.30

Use mental math to find which size is the best to buy.

A 15-oz can, since the cost per ounce for this size (about $0.057) is less than that for the 8-oz size ($0.06) or the 22-oz size ($0.059).

You may want to extend this problem by discussing why a consumer might not always buy the size that is the best bargain.

---

147 **Geometry** 3.1
Measurement 4.1
Reasoning and Proof 7.3
Communications 8.1
Representations 10.1

What is the greatest number of 4 inch by 5 inch rectangles that can be cut from a piece of material 36 inches by 54 inches? Explain how you found your answer.

97 rectangles

If the 4-in. widths are measured along the 36-in. side of the material, 90 rectangles can be cut, leaving a 4-in. by 36-in. piece of material. Seven more rectangles can be cut from this piece.

---

148 **Algebra** 2.1, 2.3
Problem Solving 6.3
Reasoning and Proof 7.2

Continue the pattern.

1, 1, 2, 3, 5, 8, ____, ____

13; 21

Each number after the second number is the sum of the two numbers before it. The sequence of numbers in this problem is called a *Fibonacci sequence.*

Answer requires writing.

| **SKILLS COVERED** | **DAILY PROBLEMS** | **TEACHER NOTES WITH ANSWERS** |

---

149   **Algebra** 2.1
Problem Solving 6.3
Reasoning and Proof 7.3

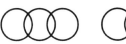 You have 5 chains, each 3 links long.

What is the least number of links you would need to open and reclose to make one chain 15 links long? Explain.

3 links

Open each link of one chain and use them to link together the other four chains.

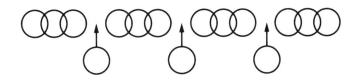

---

150   **Numbers and
   Operations** 1.2, 1.5
Algebra 2.1, 2.3
Communications 8.2
Representations 10.3

Use mental computation to solve each problem. Explain.

1. Find $\frac{1}{2}$ of 23 times 2.

2. Find $\frac{1}{3}$ of 37 times 3.

3. Find $\frac{1}{4}$ of 45 times 4.

1. 23
2. 37
3. 45

Since the commutative and associative properties hold for multiplication, the order of grouping of the factors does not change the final result. In problem 1, $\frac{1}{2}$ of 23 times 2 will have the same product as $\frac{1}{2}$ of 2 times 23. $\frac{1}{2}$ of 2 is 1, and 1 times 23 is 23. The same thinking can be used for problems 2 and 3.

	SKILLS COVERED	DAILY PROBLEMS	TEACHER NOTES WITH ANSWERS
151	**Numbers and Operations** 1.2, 1.4 **Algebra** 2.2, 2.3 **Representations** 10.3	Use the digit 9 four times to make 100.	$99 + \dfrac{9}{9}$ Encourage students to create similar problems to challenge their classmates.
152	**Geometry** 3.1 **Measurement** 4.1 **Problem Solving** 6.2, 6.3 **Representations** 10.1	Abdul is making a poster. He is using a piece of posterboard 28 inches high and 20 inches wide. He plans to make letters 2 inches high. He wants a 2-inch space left at the top, bottom, and at both sides of the poster, and a 1-inch space left between lines. What is the greatest number of lines of words Abdul can put on his poster?	8 lines Because of the 2-inch space at the top and bottom, Abdul will have 24 inches to use for lines of words plus the space between lines. The last line will use 2 inches, leaving 22 inches for the other lines plus spaces. Each other line and the space that follows it will use 3 inches. Since $22 \div 3 = 7$ R1, 7 other lines are possible. These lines plus the last line make a maximum total of 8 lines with 1 inch of space left over. Students may find it helpful to organize the information in a diagram.
153	**Measurement** 4.1, 4.2 **Reasoning and Proof** 7.1 **Communications** 8.1 **Representations** 10.1	You have only a 3-quart pitcher and a 5-quart pitcher. How can you use these to measure exactly 1 quart of water?	Fill the 3-quart pitcher with water and empty it into the 5-quart pitcher. Fill the 3-quart pitcher again and empty as much of it into the 5-quart pitcher as will fit (2 quarts). One quart will remain in the 3-quart pitcher.

✏ Answer requires writing.

SKILLS COVERED	DAILY PROBLEMS	TEACHER NOTES WITH ANSWERS

159   **Algebra** 2.1
Data Analysis 5.1
Problem Solving 6.3
Communications 8.1
Representations 10.2

There are 5 people at a meeting.

If each person shakes hands with each of the others once, how many handshakes are exchanged? Explain how you found your answer.

10 handshakes

These two strategies are very effective.

Draw a diagram.   **Use simpler problems and look for a pattern.**

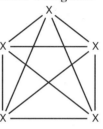
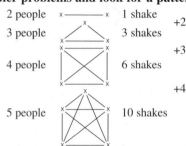

Each X represents one of the five people. Each line connecting two X's represents a handshake. Remind students that the handshake between person 1 and person 2 is the same as the handshake between person 2 and person 1.

---

160   **Algebra** 2.1
Problem Solving 6.3, 6.4

How can you arrange 4 pennies, 4 nickels, 4 dimes, and 4 quarters in this grid so that each row, each column, and each diagonal contains one of each type of coin?

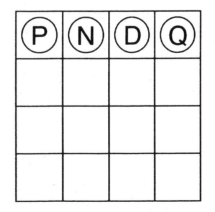

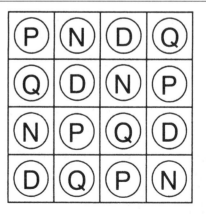

You may wish to provide students with coins or pieces of paper to arrange as they work through the problem.

 You may wish to use the standardized-test format found at the back of this manual as a review or testing option.

	SKILLS COVERED	**DAILY PROBLEMS**	**TEACHER NOTES WITH ANSWERS**

161 | **Data Analysis** 5.1 | Jenny places photos of her six closest friends in 3 rows on a poster. Greg is to the right of Amanda. Juan is between Greg and Toya. Beth is beside Juan and below Marie.

Make a sketch of the location of each photo on the poster.

Problem Solving 6.3
Representations 10.2

Marie	Toya
Beth	Juan
Amanda	Greg

Students may find it helpful to write each name on a small piece of paper and arrange and rearrange the pieces based on the information given in the problem.

---

162 | **Numbers and Operations** 1.2
Problem Solving 6.1, 6.2
Connections 9.1
Representations 10.1

At his fruit stand, Pete sells apples for 25¢ each. One day he sold three fourths of his apples and had 33 apples left.

How much money did he get paid for the apples he sold?

$24.75

This is a two-step problem. The 33 apples left represent one fourth of the apples Pete had to start with. He sold three fourths of the apples, or 3 × 33. 99 × $0.25 = $24.75.

---

163 | **Measurement** 4.2
Problem Solving 6.2, 6.3, 6.4
Reasoning and Proof 7.1

On Friday Adrianne earned half as much as she did on Thursday. On Saturday she earned twice as much as she earned on Thursday.

If her total earnings on those three days was $63, how much did she earn each day?

Adrianne's earnings were $18 on Thursday, $9 on Friday, and $36 on Saturday.

Encourage students to use guess-and-check to solve this problem. Suggest that they use a table to organize their work.

Thursday's earnings	Friday's earnings	Saturday's earnings	Total earnings
$10	$5	$20	$35
$12	$6	$24	$42
$15	$7.50	$30	$52.50
$18	$9	$36	$63

SKILLS COVERED	DAILY PROBLEMS	TEACHER NOTES WITH ANSWERS

164   **Algebra** 2.1
Data Analysis 5.3
Reasoning and Proof 7.3
Communications 8.1

Brianna has 5 pairs of gloves and 6 pairs of mittens in a drawer. On her way out of the house she reaches in the drawer without looking to pull out a pair of gloves.

How many gloves or mittens will she have to pull out before she knows for sure that she has pulled out a matching pair of gloves? Explain your answer.

18 gloves or mittens

The first 12 could all be mittens. The next 5 could be gloves that do not match. In that case, the 18th item would have to match one of the 5 gloves already pulled out.

If students have difficulty with this problem, present a simpler problem: Brianna has 2 pairs of gloves and 2 pairs of mittens. How many gloves or mittens will she have to pull out before she has a matching pair of mittens? (7; The first 4 could all be gloves. The next 2 could be mittens that do not match. The 7th item would have to match one of the mittens.)

---

165   **Measurement** 4.1
Data Analysis 5.2
Problem Solving 6.3
Connections 9.1

This table shows the number of kilometers the Mitchells drove each day of their vacation.

Find the average number of kilometers they drove each day.

Day	Distance
Sunday	190 km
Monday	260 km
Tuesday	0 km
Wednesday	245 km
Thursday	95 km

158 km

Although actual distances were only driven on 4 days, to find the average number of miles driven each day of vacation, students must divide the total distance by the total number of vacation days, or 5.

Answer requires writing.

SKILLS COVERED	DAILY PROBLEMS	TEACHER NOTES WITH ANSWERS
166 **Geometry** 3.1 **Measurement** 4.1 **Problem Solving** 6.3 **Reasoning and Proof** 7.3 **Communications** 8.1	Two rectangles have the same perimeter. Do they have the same area? Explain.	Two rectangles having the same perimeter do not necessarily have the same area. Students will most likely support their answers with examples such as the following. Perimeter: 16 units Perimeter: 16 units Area: 12 square units Area: 16 square units 2 units [rectangle] 4 units [square] 6 units 4 units
167 **Numbers and** **Operations** 1.2, 1.4 **Algebra** 2.2 **Reasoning and Proof** 7.1, 7.2	Using only the digits 6 through 9 write two fractions that have a difference close to 0. Do not use any digit more than once.	Answers will vary. *Possible answer:* $\dfrac{8}{9} - \dfrac{6}{7}$
168 **Numbers and** **Operations** 1.3, 1.5 **Measurement** 4.1, 4.2 **Reasoning and Proof** 7.1 **Connections** 9.1	Which is the better gas price, $1.52 per gallon or $0.42 per quart? Estimate to find the answer. Explain.	$1.52 per gallon Students can use 4 × $0.40 to estimate that $0.42 per quart is more expensive than $1.52 per gallon.

Answer requires writing.

SKILLS COVERED	DAILY PROBLEMS	TEACHER NOTES WITH ANSWERS

169 **Numbers and Operations** 1.1, 1.4
Algebra 2.2, 2.3
Problem Solving 6.4
Representations 10.3

The digit missing in each number is the same.

Try to find it without working the entire multiplication problem.

$$
\begin{array}{r}
48\,\square \\
\times\ 3\,\square \\
\hline
16{,}97\,\square
\end{array}
$$

5

Zero, 1, 5, and 6 are the only digits which, when multiplied by themselves, result in the same digit in the ones place of the product. By working part of the problem using zero, 1, and 6 students will find that none of these numbers could be the missing digit. Using zero will result in a zero in the tens place of the product, using 1 will result in a 1 in the tens place of the product, and using 6 will result in a 9 in the tens place of the product.

170 **Geometry** 3.1, 3.3
Problem Solving 6.3

How many triangles are in this figure?

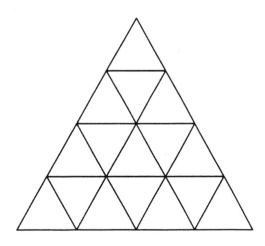

27 triangles

It may be helpful for students to organize their counting as follows:

Triangles	Number
1 row high	16
2 rows high	7
3 rows high	3
4 rows high	1
Total	27

SKILLS COVERED	DAILY PROBLEMS	TEACHER NOTES WITH ANSWERS
171 **Algebra** 2.2, 2.3 **Reasoning and Proof** 7.1 **Representations** 10.3	1. List all the factors of 32. 2. Find a number that has more factors than 32 has.	**1.** 1, 2, 4, 8, 16, 32 **2.** Answers will vary. *Possible answers:* 64 (7 factors: 1, 2, 4, 8, 16, 32, and 64) 24 (8 factors: 1, 2, 3, 4, 6, 8, 12, 24) You may want to point out that 64 is a multiple of 32. Other multiples of 32 will also have more factors than 32. If necessary, review the difference between *multiple* and *factor*.
172 **Numbers and Operations** 1.2 **Algebra** 2.4 **Problem Solving** 6.1, 6.2 **Connections** 9.2	The volleyball team played fewer than 25 games during the season and won 4 games more than it lost. The team won 70% of all its games. How many games did the team lose? Explain how you solved the problem.	3 games You may need to remind students that $70\% = \dfrac{70}{100} = \dfrac{7}{10} = \dfrac{\text{number of games won}}{\text{number of games played}}$. $10 - 7 = 3$, and 7 is 4 more than 3. 10 is less than 25. 3 is 30% of 10. The team won 7 games and lost 3 games.
173 **Numbers and Operations** 1.4 **Algebra** 2.1, 2.2 **Problem Solving** 6.2, 6.4	A jar contains 48 marbles. Each marble is yellow, blue, red, or white. There are twice as many yellow as red marbles and twice as many blue as white marbles. There are 6 more white marbles than red marbles. How many marbles of each color are there?	10 yellow, 22 blue, 5 red, and 11 white Suggest that students use the guess-and-check strategy to solve the problem. They can begin by guessing the number of red marbles and then checking the number of the other color marbles.

Answer requires writing.

SKILLS COVERED	DAILY PROBLEMS	TEACHER NOTES WITH ANSWERS

---

174 **Numbers and Operations** 1.2
Algebra 2.1
Measurement 4.2
Reasoning and Proof 7.1

The number of people seated in a theater doubled every minute.
It took 10 minutes to completely fill the theater.

How many minutes did it take for the theater to become half full?

9 minutes

It is not necessary for students to know how many people are needed to fill the theater or how many people entered the theater during the first minute. The minute before the theater is full, it must be half full.

---

175 **Geometry** 3.1
Measurement 4.1
Problem Solving 6.3
Representations 10.2

Find the surface area of this figure.

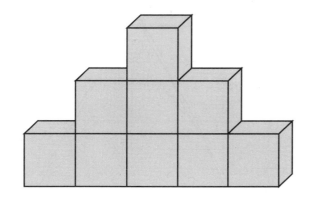

34 square units

Making a table will help students focus on each surface of this figure and keep track of the squares they have counted. Remind them that the bottom surface must be counted, too.

Surface	Number of squares
Front	9
Back	9
Bottom	5
Top	5
Left side	3
Right side	3
Total	34

SKILLS COVERED	DAILY PROBLEMS	TEACHER NOTES WITH ANSWERS

---

176   **Numbers and Operations** 1.1
Data Analysis 5.2
Problem Solving 6.2
Communications 8.1, 8.2

Suppose your math test scores are 76, 76, 83, 85, and 90.

Would you prefer the mean, median, mode, or range of these scores to be your final grade? Explain.

The median

The mean is 82, the median 83, the mode 76, and the range 14. The median is the greatest.

---

177   **Numbers and Operations** 1.4, 1.5
Algebra 2.1, 2.3
Reasoning and Proof 7.1

Change the place value of the digits in the divisor or dividend to write division problems with the following quotients. You may add zeros or move the decimal point, but you may not change the order of the digits.

$$\frac{5.4}{8)43.2}$$

1. A number between 10 and 100

2. A number between 100 and 1,000

3. A number between 0 and 5

Answers may vary. *Possible answers:*

1. $\dfrac{54}{8)432}$ **2.** $\dfrac{540}{8)4320}$ **3.** $\dfrac{0.54}{8)4.32}$

Any other answer that students can justify is acceptable.

---

178   **Numbers and Operations** 1.1
Algebra 2.1
Problem Solving 6.3
Reasoning and Proof 7.2
Communications 8.2

Solve each of these problems. Look for a pattern.

$222,222,222 \times 9 =$

$333,333,333 \times 9 =$

$444,444,444 \times 9 =$

What is the product of $999,999,999 \times 9$?

$222,222,222 \times 9 = 1,999,999,998$

$333,333,333 \times 9 = 2,999,999,997$

$444,444,444 \times 9 = 3,999,999,996$

Following the established pattern, $999,999,999 \times 9 = 8,999,999,991$.

Ask students to describe the pattern in words.

✎ Answer requires writing.

SKILLS COVERED	DAILY PROBLEMS	TEACHER NOTES WITH ANSWERS

---

179 **Numbers and Operations** 1.1
Problem Solving 6.2
Communications 8.2
Representations 10.1

The Muffin Factory made six dozen dozen bran muffins to sell on Tuesday. By Tuesday evening there were a half dozen dozen muffins left.

How many muffins had been sold that day?

792 muffins

Students may need to read this problem several times. A dozen dozen is 12×12, or 144. So, six dozen dozen is equal to $6 \times 12 \times 12$, or 864.

A half dozen dozen is equal to $\frac{1}{2}$ of 12×12, or 6×12, which is 72. Then $864 - 72 = 792$.

---

180 **Geometry** 3.1, 3.3
Measurement 4.2
Problem Solving 6.3

Suppose you have a 3 inch by 3 inch by 3 inch cube. You paint it purple. Then you cut it into 1 inch cubes as shown.

1. How many cubes have 4 sides painted purple?
2. How many cubes have 3 sides painted purple?
3. How many cubes have 2 sides painted purple?
4. How many cubes have 1 side painted purple?
5. How many cubes have 0 sides painted purple?

1. 0 cubes
2. 8 cubes
3. 12 cubes
4. 6 cubes
5. 1 cube

The visual learner may benefit from constructing a similar cube from small blocks.

You may wish to use the standardized-test format found at the back of this manual as a review or testing option.

Grade 5

DAILMathematics

Class Record Sheet

Class _____

Teacher _____

Student	1–4	5–8	9–12	13–16	17–20	21–24	25–28	29–32	33–36
1									
2									
3									
4									
5									
6									
7									
8									
9									
10									
11									
12									
13									
14									
15									
16									
17									
18									
19									
20									
21									
22									
23									
24									

Quiz for Weeks

Grade 5   DAILMathematics   *Weeks 1–4*

Name _____ Date _____

Directions: Choose the best answer to each question.

1. A digital clock shows either 3 digits or 4 digits at a time.
   At what time do the digits have the greatest sum?

   Ⓐ 12.59   Ⓑ 12:34   Ⓒ 9:99   Ⓓ 9:59

2. Juan gave two thirds of his baseball card collection to his best
   friend, Marcus. He gave one half of the cards he had left to his
   brother. Finally, he gave one half of the cards he had left to his
   sister. He had 25 cards left.

   How many cards did Juan originally have in his collection?

   Ⓐ 300 cards

   Ⓑ 200 cards

   Ⓒ 100 cards

   Ⓓ 50 cards

3. What is one hundred and seven thousandths written
   in standard form?

   Ⓐ 107.001

   Ⓑ 100.007

   Ⓒ 10.07

   Ⓓ 0.107

4. Which of these 2-digit numbers is equal to three times the product
   of its digits?

   Ⓐ 12   Ⓑ 15   Ⓒ 18   Ⓓ 25

5. Jake plans to make 12 cuts in a board. There will be a 10-inch interval
   between cuts. How long is the board?

   Ⓐ 110 in.   Ⓑ 120 in.   Ⓒ 130 in.   Ⓓ 140 in.

6. This pattern can be folded to make a cube. If the 6 is to be on the top of the cube, what number will be on the bottom?

Ⓐ 2

Ⓑ 3

Ⓒ 4

Ⓓ 5

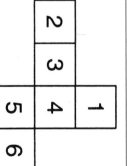

7. Jesse is 60 inches tall. That is 10 inches taller than Marie. The difference between Joe's height and Jesse's height is 2 inches more than between Joe's height and Marie's height.

How tall are Marie and Joe?

Ⓐ Marie: 54 in.; Joe: 50 in.

Ⓑ Marie: 50 in.; Joe 56 in.

Ⓒ Marie: 52 in.; Joe: 54 in.

Ⓓ Marie: 50 in.; Joe: 54 in.

8. How many different 3-digit numbers can you write using the digits 0, 2, 4, and 6? Use a digit only once in a number.

Ⓐ 12 numbers

Ⓑ 16 numbers

Ⓒ 18 numbers

Ⓓ 24 numbers

9. Chantel made a display of video-game cartridges. There are 3 games in the top row. There are 3 more cartridges in each row than in the row above it. If the display has 8 rows, how many cartridges did Chantel use?

Ⓐ 81 cartridges

Ⓑ 105 cartridges

Ⓒ 108 cartridges

Ⓓ 115 cartridges

10. Lerna has two coins that total 30¢. What are the two coins if one coin is not a nickel?

Ⓐ a quarter and a nickel

Ⓑ a quarter and a dime

Ⓒ two quarters

Ⓓ two dimes

Answer Key, Weeks 5–8

1. C
2. B
3. C
4. A
5. B

6. B
7. C
8. C
9. D
10. B

Name _____ Date _____

Directions: Choose the best answer to each question.

1. Dustin bowled games with scores of 120, 116, and 127. What was his average?

   (A) 119   (B) 120   (C) 121   (D) 127

2. In professional football, a team can score in the following ways:

Type of Play	Points
Touchdown	6
Field goal	3
Safety	2
Point after touchdown	1

   During a game a team scores a total of 20 points. They score 2 touchdowns. Which of the following is **not** a way they could score the remaining points?

   (A) 2 field goals, 1 safety, 0 points after touchdown

   (B) 1 field goal, 1 safety, 2 points after touchdown

   (C) 0 field goals, 4 safeties, 0 points after touchdown

   (D) 0 field goals, 3 safeties, 2 points after touchdown

3. What is the area of a square whose perimeter is 24 inches?

   (A) 24 square in.   (C) 36 square in.

   (B) 32 square in.   (D) 48 square in.

4. Choose the correct answer without working the problem. $327 \div 6 =$

   (A) 54 R3   (C) 55 R7

   (B) 54 R6   (D) 55 R9

5. A package of plastic forks contains 8 forks. A package of plastic knives contains 12 knives. What is the fewest number of packages you would have to buy to have exactly the same number of forks as knives?

   (A) 2 packages of forks and 1 of knives   (C) 6 packages of forks and 4 of knives

   (B) 3 packages of forks and 2 of knives   (D) 12 packages of forks and 8 of knives

Name _____

6. The Wildcats' average score for three basketball games is 76. They scored 70 and 84 in the first two games. What score did they have in the third game?

Ⓐ 72   Ⓑ 74   Ⓒ 76   Ⓓ 78

7. How many small cubes are in this block?

Ⓐ 9 cubes

Ⓑ 16 cubes

Ⓒ 27 cubes

Ⓓ 36 cubes

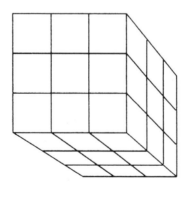

8. What number are you most likely to land on if you spin the spinner?

Ⓐ 1

Ⓑ 2

Ⓒ 3

Ⓓ They are all equally likely.

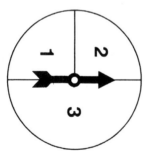

9. Yani has between 50 and 100 pennies in her collection. When she divides them into groups of 2, of 3, or of 7, there is always 1 penny left. How many pennies does Yani have in her collection?

Ⓐ 42 pennies   Ⓑ 65 pennies   Ⓒ 79 pennies   Ⓓ 85 pennies

10. A pencil and an eraser cost 40¢. If the pencil costs 30¢ more than the eraser, what is the cost of the eraser?

Ⓐ 3¢   Ⓑ 5¢   Ⓒ 10¢   Ⓓ 15¢

Grade 5   DAILYMathematics   *Weeks 9–12*

Name _____ Date _____

Directions: Choose the best answer to each question.

1. What is the area of this figure?

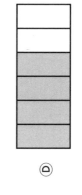

Ⓐ 200 in.   Ⓒ 132 in.

Ⓑ 168 in.   Ⓓ 68 in.

2. Each of the three rectangles is the same shape and size. What is the perimeter of the figure?

Ⓐ 40 cm   Ⓒ 60 cm

Ⓑ 47 cm   Ⓓ 63 cm

3. Which picture does **not** show a representation of $\frac{4}{3}$?

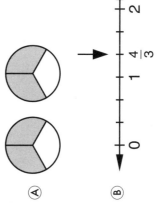

4. A clock strikes once at 1:00, twice at 2:00, and so on. Also, it strikes once at half past each hour. How many times will the clock strike during one 12-hour period?

Ⓐ 33 times   Ⓑ 78 times   Ⓒ 90 times   Ⓓ 180 times

5. The number of students on the field trip is greater than 30 but less than 50. When seated 2 in a seat on the bus, no student has to sit alone. When placed in groups of 5 for a tour, all groups are the same size. How many students are on the field trip?

Ⓐ 20 students   Ⓑ 40 students   Ⓒ 35 students   Ⓓ 48 students

6. Jessica has a softball game every 3 days. She has a piano lesson every 7 days. Every fourth day it is her turn to wash the dishes after supper. Today Jessica has a softball game and piano lesson, and it is her turn to wash the dishes. How soon will these three activities occur again on the same day?

   Ⓐ in 28 days   Ⓑ in 42 days   Ⓒ in 63 days   Ⓓ in 84 days

7. Which of the following sets of symbols, used in order, would **not** make a true sentence with these numbers?

   3 2 5 4 2 2 = 6

   Ⓐ $+ - + + -$ Ⓑ $+ + - - +$ Ⓒ $- + + - -$ Ⓓ $+ + - + -$

8. Use mental computation to identify the problem that has a product of 3,286.

   Ⓐ 51×64 Ⓑ 42×93 Ⓒ 53×62 Ⓓ 38×77

9. How many squares are there in this figure?

   Ⓐ 16 squares

   Ⓑ 21 squares

   Ⓒ 25 squares

   Ⓓ 30 squares

10. At a red light, 2 cars are stopped in front of a car, and 2 cars are stopped behind a car. What is the fewest number of cars that could be stopped at the red light?

   Ⓐ 2 cars   Ⓑ 3 cars   Ⓒ 4 cars   Ⓓ 5 cars

Grade 5 **DAILMathematics** *Weeks 13–16*

Name _____ Date _____

Directions: Choose the best answer to each question.

---

1. What is the next number in each of these patterns?

   12, 10, 15, 13, 18, 16, 21, _____
   1, 2, 4, 5, 10, 11, 22, 23, _____

   Ⓐ 26; 46   Ⓑ 19; 24   Ⓒ 19; 46   Ⓓ 26; 24

---

2. For dessert you can choose apple, cherry, blueberry, or peach pie, and milk or juice to drink. How many different combinations can you choose from?

   Ⓐ 4 combinations   Ⓑ 5 combinations   Ⓒ 6 combinations   Ⓓ 8 combinations

---

3. The area of a rectangular dog pen is 48 square feet. The length of each side is a whole number. What is the least perimeter the pen could have?

   Ⓐ 14 ft   Ⓑ 28 ft   Ⓒ 32 ft   Ⓓ 38 ft

---

4. At 6:00 P.M. the temperature was 14°F. By midnight, the temperature had fallen to −4°F. How many degrees did the temperature fall?

   Ⓐ 10°   Ⓑ 14°   Ⓒ 18°   Ⓓ 24°

---

5. The total cost of a model plane and a model boat is $15.
   The total cost of 3 model planes and 2 model boats is $37.

   What is the cost of a model plane?

   Ⓐ $7   Ⓑ $6.50   Ⓒ $5   Ⓓ $4

---

6. If the area of each small square is 10 square centimeters, what is the area of the entire figure?

   Ⓐ 50 square centimeters
   Ⓑ 120 square centimeters
   Ⓒ 300 square centimeters
   Ⓓ 240 square centimeters

7. This map shows the streets in downtown Centerville. If traffic is only allowed to go north or east on these streets, how many different routes could a person follow to drive from the library to the park?

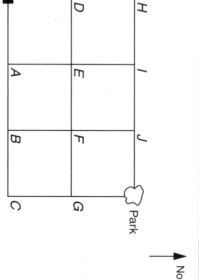

Library   North

Ⓐ 1 route   Ⓒ 8 routes

Ⓑ 5 routes   Ⓓ 10 routes

8. Lines *a*, *b*, and *c* are in the same plane. Line *a* is perpendicular to line *b*. Line *a* is parallel to line *c*.

How are line *b* and line *c* related?

Ⓐ perpendicular   Ⓒ askew

Ⓑ parallel   Ⓓ crossing, but not perpendicular

9. There are 8 teams. Suppose you set up a single-elimination tournament to determine a winner. How many games will it take before a winner is determined, and how many games would the winning team play?

Ⓐ 15; 7   Ⓑ 8; 4   Ⓒ 7; 4   Ⓓ 7; 3

10. Derek, Shana, Curt, and Lela are brothers and sisters. Each plays one of the following instruments: piano, drums, clarinet, and trumpet. Derek's brother does not use his mouth when playing his instrument. One of Derek's sisters plays the clarinet. Lela is glad she will never have to march in a parade playing her instrument. Which instrument does each person play?

Ⓐ Derek: drums; Shana: clarinet; Curt: trumpet; Lela: piano

Ⓑ Derek: clarinet; Shana: trumpet; Curt: piano; Lela: drums

Ⓒ Derek: trumpet; Shana: clarinet; Curt: drums; Lela: piano

Ⓓ Derek: piano; Shana: trumpet; Curt: drums; Lela: clarinet

Answer Key, Weeks 17–20

1. C
2. D
3. B
4. A
5. C

6. C
7. A
8. B
9. D
10. C

Name _____   Date _____

Directions: Choose the best answer to each question.

1. The range of a baseball team's scores for four games is 9. The scores for three games are 5, 3, and 8. What is the score for the fourth game?

   Ⓐ 4   Ⓑ 9   Ⓒ 12   Ⓓ 15

2. Find each quotient. Look for a pattern.

   $21 \div 3 =$
   $201 \div 3 =$
   $2,001 \div 3 =$

   Use the pattern you found. What is the quotient of $200,001 \div 3$?

   Ⓐ 667   Ⓑ 6,677   Ⓒ 6,667   Ⓓ 66,667

3. In the Ortez family, there is a grandmother and a grandfather. There are also 4 mothers and 2 fathers. Half of the mothers have 3 daughters and half have 1 daughter. Half of the fathers have 2 sons and half have 1 son.

   What is the fewest number of people there could be in the Ortez family?

   Ⓐ 11 people   Ⓑ 13 people   Ⓒ 15 people   Ⓓ 19 people

4. Which of the following does **not** show 4 equal parts?

   Ⓐ   Ⓑ   Ⓒ   Ⓓ

5. On their vacation the Chins plan to visit a museum, a beach, and an amusement park. They have their choice of a science, a history, or an art museum; a beach on the ocean or at a lake; and a water-ride park or a park with a giant roller coaster.

   In how many ways can the Chins visit a museum, then a beach, and finally an amusement park?

   Ⓐ 7 ways   Ⓑ 10 ways   Ⓒ 12 ways   Ⓓ 15 ways

6. Complete each problem. Look for a pattern. Use the pattern you discovered to find the missing number.

   $1 \times 9 + 2 =$
   $12 \times 9 + 3 =$
   $123 \times 9 + 4 =$
   _____ $\times 9 + 8 = 11,111,111$

   Ⓐ 123,456　　Ⓑ 123,123　　Ⓒ 1,234,567　　Ⓓ 12,345,678

7. Maria ran 450 yards. Brittany ran $\frac{1}{4}$ mile. Who ran farther? How much farther?

   Ⓐ Maria ran 10 yards farther.

   Ⓑ Brittany ran 10 yards farther.

   Ⓒ Maria ran 20 feet farther.

   Ⓓ Brittany ran 20 feet farther.

8. You have 8 white socks and 8 blue socks in your drawer. You reach in without looking and pull out one sock at a time. What is the fewest number of socks you would need to take out to be sure you got a matching pair?

   Ⓐ 2 socks　　Ⓑ 3 socks　　Ⓒ 8 socks　　Ⓓ 9 socks

9. Which of the following sentences is not true?

   Ⓐ $404 \div 4 = 101$　　Ⓑ $2 \times 356 = 712$　　Ⓒ $427 - 9 = 418$　　Ⓓ $678 \div 9 = 156$

10. The combined ages of Joel, his father, and his grandfather are equal to 100. Joel is 25 years younger than his father and 51 years younger than his grandfather. How old are Joel, his father, and his grandfather?

    Ⓐ 1, 26, 52　　Ⓑ 5, 30, 56　　Ⓒ 8, 33, 59　　Ⓓ 11, 36, 53

Answer Key, Weeks 21–24

1. C   6. D
2. B   7. C
3. D   8. C
4. B   9. B
5. A   10. A

Name _____ Date _____

Directions: Choose the best answer to each question.

1. $5.58 + 3.26 =$ _____

   Ⓐ 2.32   Ⓑ 8.82   Ⓒ 8.84   Ⓓ 88.4

2. What must the temperature be on Friday to have a 5-day average of 42°F?

   Ⓐ 40°F
   Ⓑ 41°F
   Ⓒ 42°F
   Ⓓ 43°F

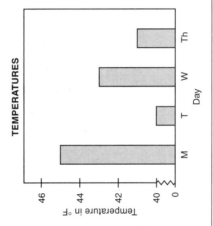

TEMPERATURES

Temperature in °F

46, 44, 42, 40, 0

M T W Th

Day

3. What is the least fraction you can write using the digits 3, 4, and 5 each only once?

   Ⓐ $\frac{3}{45}$ Ⓑ $\frac{5}{43}$ Ⓒ $\frac{4}{53}$ Ⓓ $\frac{3}{54}$

4. There are rectangular tables in the school cafeteria. Two students can sit on each side, and one student can sit at each end. How many tables need to be pushed together to form one long table that will seat 34?

   Ⓐ 7 tables   Ⓑ 8 tables   Ⓒ 12 tables   Ⓓ 15 tables

5. What is the area of the figure?

   Ⓐ 8 square units
   Ⓑ 9 square units
   Ⓒ 12 square units
   Ⓓ 16 square units

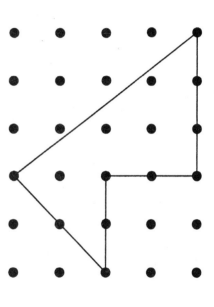

6. On the hour, a clock chimes once for each hour. Each chime lasts
   1 second, and there is a $\frac{1}{2}$-second rest between chimes. How long
   does it take this clock to chime for 6:00?

   Ⓐ 6 seconds   Ⓑ $6\frac{1}{2}$ seconds   Ⓒ $7\frac{1}{2}$ seconds   Ⓓ $8\frac{1}{2}$ seconds

7. Which of the following pairs of numbers
   does **not** show the function applied correctly?

   Ⓐ In 4: Out 9

   Ⓑ In 1: Out 3

   Ⓒ In 7: Out 13

   Ⓓ In 5: Out 11

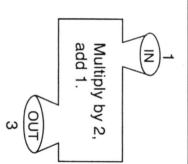

8. A fathom is a unit of measure equivalent to 6 feet.
   How many fathoms are in a mile?

   Ⓐ 297 fathoms   Ⓑ 440 fathoms   Ⓒ 880 fathoms   Ⓓ 1760 fathoms

9. What is the surface area of a cube whose sides have lengths of 5 inches?

   Ⓐ 125 square inches

   Ⓑ 150 square inches

   Ⓒ 160 square inches

   Ⓓ 180 square inches

10. A cereal company puts a 25¢-off coupon in every other box of cereal it
    packages. It puts a pencil in every fifth box. It puts a coupon for a free
    gallon of milk in every eighth box.

    Out of the first 100 boxes, how many will have a 25¢-off coupon,
    a pencil, and a coupon for a free gallon of milk?

    Ⓐ 2 boxes   Ⓑ 10 boxes   Ⓒ 20 boxes   Ⓓ 40 boxes

Grade 5 **DAILMathematics** *Weeks 25–28*

Name _____ Date _____

Directions: Choose the best answer to each question.

1. It takes 4 carpenters 4 minutes to nail 4 boards in place. At this rate, how long will it take 80 carpenters to nail 80 boards in place?

   Ⓐ 1 minute   Ⓑ 4 minutes   Ⓒ 20 minutes   Ⓓ 80 minutes

2. Solve each of these problems. Look for a pattern.

   $37 \times 3 =$ $37 \times 6 =$ $37 \times 9 =$

   What is the product of 37×27?

   Ⓐ 777   Ⓑ 888   Ⓒ 999   Ⓓ 1,111

3. Which of the following number substitutions would **not** make the equation true?

   $\triangle + \square + \square = 9$

   Ⓐ $\triangle = 2;\ \square = 3$

   Ⓑ $\triangle = 7;\ \square = 1$

   Ⓒ $\triangle = 5;\ \square = 2$

   Ⓓ $\triangle = 1;\ \square = 4$

4. Ben is building a fence. He places 15 fence posts 8 feet apart. What is the distance from the first fence post to the last?

   Ⓐ 105 feet   Ⓑ 112 feet   Ⓒ 120 feet   Ⓓ 128 feet

5. Which formula would you use to determine how many seconds you sleep each night?

   Ⓐ number of hours $\times$ 60

   Ⓑ number of hours $\times$ 120

   Ⓒ number of hours $\times$ 60 $\times$ 60

   Ⓓ number of hours $\times$ 60 $\times$ 60 $\times$ 60

6. At the end of the track meet Team A had 5 points less than Team B. Team D had 15 points more than Team A. Team B had 15 more points than Team C.

What was the order of finish?

Ⓐ A, B, C, D   Ⓑ B, D, C, A   Ⓒ C, A, B, D   Ⓓ D, B, A, C

7. How many squares are in this figure?

Ⓐ 7 squares

Ⓑ 9 squares

Ⓒ 12 squares

Ⓓ 15 squares

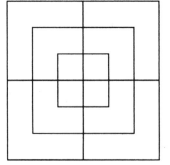

8. Arrange these numbers in order, from least to greatest.

$$0.5 \qquad \frac{3}{5} \qquad 0.45 \qquad \frac{4}{20}$$

Ⓐ $\frac{4}{20}, 0.45, 0.5, \frac{3}{5}$ Ⓑ $0.5, \frac{3}{5}, 0.45, \frac{4}{20}$ Ⓒ $\frac{3}{5}, 0.5, 0.45, \frac{4}{20}$ Ⓓ $\frac{4}{20}, \frac{3}{5}, 0.45, 0.5$

9. A rectangle has a perimeter of 30 cm. The length and width are each whole numbers. What is the greatest possible area the rectangle could have?

Ⓐ 54 square centimeters

Ⓑ 56 square centimeters

Ⓒ 225 square centimeters

Ⓓ 300 square centimeters

10. Five flags are spaced evenly around a track. It took a runner 30 seconds to get from the first flag to the third flag. If the runner continues at the same speed, how long will it take her to get completely around the track?

Ⓐ 50 seconds

Ⓑ 60 seconds

Ⓒ 75 seconds

Ⓓ 90 seconds

Answer Key, Weeks 29–32

1. A
2. C
3. B
4. C
5. B

6. C
7. A
8. B
9. A
10. C

Grade 5 **DAILYMathematics** *Weeks 29–32*

Name _____ Date _____

Directions: Choose the best answer to each question.

1. What two numbers continue the pattern?

   1, 1, 2, 3, 5, 8, _____, _____

   (A) 13; 21 (B) 11; 19 (C) 12; 17 (D) 15; 23

2. This quadrilateral has two diagonals.
   What polygon has 20 diagonals?

   (A) hexagon (C) octagon
   (B) heptagon (D) nonagon

3. You have 5 chains, each 3 links long.

   What is the least number of links you would need to open and reclose
   to make one chain 15 links long?

   (A) 2 links (B) 3 links (C) 4 links (D) 5 links

4. Whitney has between 50 and 100 coins in her collection. Three eighths
   of them are U.S. coins. One tenth of the U.S. coins are nickels. How
   many coins are in Whitney's collection?

   (A) 56 coins (B) 64 coins (C) 80 coins (D) 95 coins

5. Identify the problem that has a reasonable answer.

   (A) $3.46 \times 4 = 138.4$
   (B) $5,282 \div 38 = 139$
   (C) $48.2 \times 5 = 28.92$
   (D) $4,136 \div 52 = 709 \text{ R28}$

6. There are 5 people at a meeting. If each person shakes hands with each of the others once, how many handshakes are exchanged?

   Ⓐ 4 handshakes   Ⓒ 10 handshakes

   Ⓑ 5 handshakes   Ⓓ 20 handshakes

7. Abdul is making a poster. He is using a piece of posterboard 28 inches high and 20 inches wide. He plans to make letters 2 inches high. He wants a 2-inch space left at the top, bottom, and at both sides of the poster, and a 1-inch space left between lines. What is the greatest number of lines of words Abdul can put on his poster?

   Ⓐ 8 lines   Ⓑ 9 lines   Ⓒ 12 lines   Ⓓ 14 lines

8. Which net cannot be folded to form a rectangular prism?

Ⓐ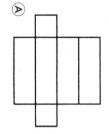

Ⓑ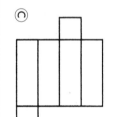

Ⓒ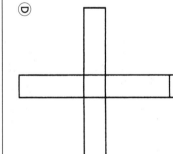

Ⓓ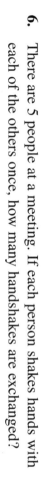

9. Use mental computation to identify the correct answer to 14.3 − 9.476.

   Ⓐ 4.824   Ⓑ 4.976   Ⓒ 5.176   Ⓓ 23.776

10. What is the greatest number of 4 inch by 5 inch rectangles that can be cut from a piece of material 36 inches by 54 inches?

   Ⓐ 88 rectangles   Ⓒ 97 rectangles

   Ⓑ 90 rectangles   Ⓓ 99 rectangles

Grade 5   DAILMathematics   *Weeks 33–36*

Name _____ Date _____

Directions: Choose the best answer to each question.

1. Suppose your math test scores are 76, 76, 83, 85, and 90. Would you prefer the mean, median, mode, or range of these scores to be your final grade?

   Ⓐ mean   Ⓑ median   Ⓒ mode   Ⓓ range

2. Find the surface area of this figure.

   Ⓐ 17 square units
   Ⓑ 20 square units
   Ⓒ 29 square units
   Ⓓ 34 square units

3. How many triangles are in this figure?

   Ⓐ 27 triangles
   Ⓑ 25 triangles
   Ⓒ 22 triangles
   Ⓓ 16 triangles

4. The Muffin Factory made six dozen dozen bran muffins to sell on Tuesday. By Tuesday evening there were a half dozen dozen muffins left. How many muffins had been sold that day?

   Ⓐ 66 muffins   Ⓒ 858 muffins
   Ⓑ 792 muffins   Ⓓ 864 muffins

5. This table shows the number of kilometers the Mitchells drove each day of their vacation. Find the average number of kilometers they drove each day.

   Ⓐ 95 km
   Ⓑ 158 km
   Ⓒ 198 km
   Ⓓ 245 km

Day	Distance
Sunday	190 km
Monday	260 km
Tuesday	0 km
Wednesday	245 km
Thursday	95 km

6. Brianna has 5 pairs of gloves and 6 pairs of mittens in a drawer. On her way out of the house she reaches in the drawer without looking to pull out a pair of gloves. How many gloves or mittens will she have to pull out before she knows for sure that she has pulled out a matching pair of gloves?

(A) 6 gloves or mittens

(B) 11 gloves or mittens

(C) 13 gloves or mittens

(D) 18 gloves or mittens

7. Solve each of these problems. Look for a pattern.

$222{,}222{,}222 \times 9 = \qquad 333{,}333{,}333 \times 9 = \qquad 444{,}444{,}444 \times 9 =$

What is the product of $999{,}999{,}999 \times 9$?

(A) 10,000,009

(B) 9,999,999,990

(C) 8,999,999,991

(D) 7,999,999,992

8. The volleyball team played less than 25 games during the season and won 4 games more than it lost. The team won 70% of all its games. How many games did the team lose?

(A) 3 games

(B) 4 games

(C) 7 games

(D) 10 games

9. The digit missing in each number is the same. What is it?

$$\begin{array}{r} 48\square \\ \times\ 3\square \\ \hline 16{,}97\square \end{array}$$

(A) 0

(B) 1

(C) 2

(D) 5

10. At his fruit stand, Pete sells apples for 25¢ each. One day he sold three fourths of his apples and had 33 apples left. How much money did he get paid for the apples he sold?

(A) $8.25

(B) $16.50

(C) $24.75

(D) $33.00